First Time
Resume

by
William McNeill

Adams Media Corporation

Holbrook, Massachusetts

I would like to thank Bob Adams and Mark Lipsman
for their help with this book.

———————————————

Published by
Adams Media Corporation
260 Center Street, Holbrook, MA 02343. U.S.A.

ISBN: 1-58062-292-5

Printed in Canada.

JIHGFEDCBA

Library of Congress Cataloging-in-Publication Data
McNeill, William
First time resume / William McNeill.
p.   cm.
ISBN 1-58062-292-5
1. Resumes (Employment)
HF5383 .M232   2000
650.14—dc21   99-087977
CIP

This publication is designed to provide accurate and authoritative information with regard to the subject matter covered. It is sold with the understanding that the publisher is not engaged in rendering legal,
accounting, or other professional advice. If legal advice or other expert assistance is required, the services of a competent professional person should be sought.
    — From a *Declaration of Principles* jointly adopted by a Committee of the American Bar
                          Association and a Committee of Publishers and Associations

This book is available at quantity discounts for bulk purchases.
For information, call 1-800-872-5627.

Visit our exciting Web site at www.careercity.com

CONTENTS

PREFACE

Whether you're a high school student or a seasoned professional, anyone can use *First Time Resume* to write a winning resume. This book is designed to be easy to use, yet informative and powerful. I want to show you that creating a winning resume really can be easy; it just takes some time and effort.

Not only does this book teach you how to craft a winning resume, it contains detailed information about the best ways to find a job, how to network, how to job search in today's high-tech world, how to create an electronic resume you can e-mail or post on the Internet, how to write an effective cover letter, and what to expect on a job interview.

This isn't just another book stuffed cover to cover with outdated resumes. The resumes in this book are streamlined and up to date. Plus, I've added comments to each one to show you exactly why it's a winner.

And I'm not going to waste your money by including dozens of blank pages calling them "worksheets" or "forms." No one actually uses those things. When you get to the section on creating your resume, get out some paper and a pen and use that to write your draft.

With *First Time Resume* as your guide, you'll have a professional-looking resume and cover letter, you'll know what employers are looking for, and you'll understand how to go about a successful job search.

INTRODUCTION

As a rule, the best jobs do not necessarily go to the most qualified individuals; they generally go to the best job hunters or the people with connections. This is a vitally important point, especially if you are competing for an entry-level position. Even though you may compete with people who have stronger credentials, you can still get the job you want if you're willing to put in the extra effort and energy necessary to outshine the competition.

WHAT TO EXPECT

A company will often consider dozens, if not hundreds, of individuals for the typical entry-level position! Clearly, then, it is in your best interest to unearth every imaginable employment opportunity. You will need to apply to many companies to turn the odds in your favor. Too many people study in school for seventeen years and then accept the first job offer that comes their way. You don't have to do that, especially if you are ready to put plenty of work into your job search campaign—and begin as soon as possible.

But be forewarned: getting even one job offer will be tough. Some people send out hundreds of resumes without getting a response. Personally, I've never had that problem, but it seems that most job search books say that, and I bet if you think hard enough you can think of someone who has been in that position. I think that if you're sending out hundreds of resumes and not getting a response, it doesn't mean you're not a good candidate, it just means you need to fine tune *how* you're looking for a job.

If you're really serious about job searching, if you're serious about your career, you need to understand that searching for a job can be a job itself. Don't be discouraged. This book is loaded with great information all designed to give you that extra edge over the competition. Success will not go to the job hunter who invests little effort, becomes discouraged, and takes the first job possibility that comes around. Remember, the time you put into your job search will be time well spent if you make sure all of that effort and energy is going in the right direction.

Remember, you'll probably spend more time at work than you will at home! So it's important that you take the time to find a job you'll like.

STANDING OUT FROM THE PACK

You can increase your chances of landing a great job by standing out from the pack. You must demonstrate that in addition to fulfilling the basic requirements, there are some special reasons you deserve extra consideration. I'll show you how to do exactly that—and more—in the pages ahead.

CHAPTER ONE

The Qualities Employers Look For

You may be surprised to learn that employers generally are not looking for just the smartest person, or the person with the most recommendations. One of the most important things that employers are particularly concerned about is the answer to a simple question: How long will you stay with the company?

COMMITMENT

The average college grad, for example, only stays with his or her first employer for nine months. And remember, that's an average; half of the people who are hired stay for less than nine months! Employers have concluded that most new young hires are unrealistic about what entry-level jobs entail and will soon leave in search of something better. They're right.

This cycle costs companies a lot of money, because training new hires is very expensive. Some companies and large corporations might spend as much as $60,000 per new employee in training programs over the first six months. If you leave after nine months, the firm will lose its investment. It's not surprising, then, that most companies—especially those with training programs—will be very interested in whether you are likely to remain in that position for a period of time.

How can you show a company that you won't move on too soon? You must display a true interest in the industry, in the job function itself, and particularly in that employer. Intelligently discussing current trends in the industry and showing that you are genuinely interested in the job are two great ways to communicate to an interviewer that you're a low-risk hire.

If you're a student, another way to demonstrate this is to stress only a small number of extracurricular activities that you pursued for an extended period of time: this shows that you didn't just participate in many different activities, jumping from one to the next.

Although this may seem surprising, it may actually look better to an employer if you participated in only one activity during your college career than if you experimented with many. As long as the activity you highlight was something you spent a lot of time and energy doing, something you made progress in over the years, it will carry more weight than many activities that you were only nominally involved in. Remember, consistency is often more important to employers than excellence in school or outside activities. The concept of consistency is one that I will be stressing throughout this book.

Additionally, you should show the employer that you're likely to stay with the firm by making it clear that you know what you want. Although you probably don't know the precise title of the job you want, you must show the employer some particular interests and career direction.

You should also show that you have a realistic feeling for what the job entails, that you understand what the pluses and minuses are of the position you are considering, and that you've decided, after making a realistic assessment of the job, that it's something you would enjoy doing for a substantial period of time.

MATURITY AND CONFIDENCE

Another factor that employers weigh heavily is maturity. Many young people, in one-to-one situations with older adults, simply don't come across as being mature and confident enough for the professional world. Unfortunately, such judgments are often made based on a brief one-on-one interview. Your references could help you in some cases, but your interview is going to matter much more. Later on in this book, I'll talk about how you can prepare for your interviews and how you can make sure that you project yourself as a candidate who is mature and ready to enter the business community. If you're older, great, then you probably already know what I'm talking about.

PROFESSIONALISM

Employers will also want to know whether or not you have a professional demeanor. This demeanor is difficult to define, but it is perhaps best understood as the ability to fit in with others in a given work group, adhering to their standards of communication, dress, and conduct. Your professionalism is something you need to prove to employers as soon as you contact their firm.

One of the ways you show a company this, of course, is by following an accepted format for your resume. Your cover letter also needs to look professional. (We'll review all the details later in the book.) In terms of dress, it is important that you look like you will fit in at the company from the very first glimpse. In your answers and presentation at the job interview, you must convey that you know how to conduct yourself properly in a business setting.

ADAPTABILITY AND GROWTH

Proving you can do a certain job is not enough. Companies, especially those hiring for management training programs, also want to see that you are going to grow within the company. Employers hope to use these programs to groom potential future senior managers. You must assure them that you are capable of adapting to new positions within the company and that you can handle a good deal of responsibility.

BUT THAT'S NOT ALL!

Punctuality is a sign of responsibility. You have to be on time for the interview. (Many people show up late!) What's more, you will have to project the image of a business-oriented person by showing an interest in the industry and in the business world in general. To be sure, employers also want a reasonably high degree of certainty that you can perform the job function. But because most people applying for an entry-level position aren't going to be able to prove their capabilities by citing lots of previous professional work experience, elements such as punctuality and professionalism are crucial in applying for that first job. I don't care if you're applying to be president of the company or the janitor, all the best candidates approach the job search and interview process with a good sense of professionalism.

In short, employers are looking for applicants who are likely to stay with their company for a reasonable length of time, have some career direction, and are interested not only in the job itself, but the industry as well. Recruiters seek applicants who are realistic about the job they're applying for. They like to see people who are mature, confident, responsible, and professional. Lastly, employers seek applicants who are ready and eager to enter the business world and who will grow within their company and contribute to its success.

You may feel the temptation at this point to pick up the phone or mail letters in hopes of securing the interviews at which you can project these qualities. Before you do, however, you will need to focus your search, and you will need to take a good look at the specific "package" you will offer the employer. Your resume and cover letter help complete that package. That's what this book is all about.

CHAPTER TWO

The Best Ways to Find a Job (and the Worst!)

You may be surprised to learn that some of the most popular job-search methods are quite unsuccessful for most of the people who use them. In this chapter, you'll have a chance to take a look at the real value of the major techniques at your disposal.

NEWSPAPER ADS

Are newspaper ads a good source of opportunities for those entering the job market? The conventional wisdom is no. It seems to be all the rage to say don't bother using newspaper ads to find a job. The experts say that your resume will just get lost in the deluge of resumes the company receives from that ad. My conclusion is that it can be hit or miss depending on your situation and the type of industry you are in.

For example, I found my best job through the newspaper. I was told that one of the reasons I stood out was because of my resume! So in this case, I stood out from the pack. But you might say, Well, all those other people *didn't* get the job. You're right. But I know many other people at my company who also got their jobs through the newspaper. So it's clear that it works for some people.

To let you make the best decision on this matter, I will present the case against using the newspaper. Department of Labor statistics show that most people do not get their jobs through newspaper ads.

One of the reasons newspapers are not a good source for job opportunities is that once a company advertises a job opening in a newspaper, it is deluged with hundreds of applications. This is often quite disruptive; a company will typically try anything and everything to fill a job opening before resorting to listing it in the classified section. This means that there are very few job openings listed in the newspaper relative to the actual number of jobs available at any given time.

There's more bad news. By the time a job is listed in the classified ads, there's a good chance the position has already been filled or is close to being filled. Even if the position is still available by the time the company receives your resume, the competition will be so fierce that your chances of getting an interview will be quite small.

For all of these reasons, relying solely on newspaper ads is usually a very tough way to get a job. Note that I said *solely*. This is not to say that you should ignore promising opportunities you see advertised, but you certainly shouldn't make scanning the want ads your only research activity.

I recommend doing a little research on the company whose ad you are answering. Find out as much as you can. This will help you write an informed, detailed cover letter. If you make it to the interview stage, it will show that you're an informed candidate who did your homework.

In summary, I recommend that you use several avenues of attack, newspaper ads being one of them. While you're sending out resumes in response to advertisements, you should also be using some of the other methods discussed in this chapter.

PROFESSIONAL EMPLOYMENT AGENCIES

Should you work with professional employment agencies? Again, this method, like many others, can be hit or miss. I have friends who have found great jobs within two weeks by using these services. Personally, I have not had the same results. Despite my professional qualifications, I was often steered toward jobs for which I was overqualified or those that were not even close to what I was looking for.

These agencies have traditionally focused on either secretarial and administrative positions or on highly specialized professional openings intended for people with a great deal of professional experience. If you fall into either of these categories, then a professional employment agency could probably help you.

Many people who use employment agencies wind up in a job that they really didn't want in the first place. Virtually all employment agencies are paid for by the employer. It's not surprising, then, that the employment agency is going to be much more responsive to the needs of the employer than to your needs.

If you decide to use an agency, you need to make sure of one very important point: make sure the employers pay the fees. With so many jobs, there really is no reason why you should ever pay a fee to someone to help you find a job. Most agencies don't charge fees, but there's no harm in asking.

There are four places to find a good agency. First, ask any friends and family members if they've used one they like. Second, look in the newspaper classifieds just as you would looking for a job on your own. Many employment agencies advertise in this section and you'll be able to get a good idea of what type of positions they are filling. The third place to look is in the Yellow Pages. The fourth place to look is in a book like the *Adams Executive Recruiters Almanac*, which lists career counseling services as well as executive search firms, employment agencies, and temporary help services located throughout the United States. This guide may be found in bookstores, your local library, or your college career office.

When you do find one you want to contact, make sure they fill positions in the areas you are looking. If you're looking for secretarial and administrative support positions, this method should work reasonably well for you.

COMMUNITY AGENCIES

Many nonprofit organizations offer counseling, career development, and job placement services. Often these services are targeted to a particular group, for example women, minorities, the blind, and the disabled. Many cities and towns have commissions that provide services for these special groups. The following national organizations provide information on career planning, training, or public policy support for specific groups.

For Women
U.S. Department of Labor
Women's Bureau
200 Constitution Avenue NW
Washington, DC 20210
Phone: (202) 219-6606

Wider Opportunities for Women
815 15th St. N.W.
Suite 916
Washington, DC 20005
Phone: (202) 638-3143

For Minorities
National Association for the Advancement of Colored People (NAACP)
Attn: Job Services
4805 Mt. Hope Drive
Baltimore, MD 21215
Phone: (410) 358-8900

National Urban League
Employment Department
120 Wall Street, 8th Floor
New York, NY 10005
Phone: (212) 558-5300

National Urban League
Washington Operations
1111 14th Street NW
Suite 1001
Washington, DC 20005
Phone: (202) 898-1604

For the Blind

Job Opportunities for the Blind Program
National Federation of the Blind
1800 Johnson Street
Baltimore, MD 21230
Phone: (410) 659-9314

For the Disabled

President's Committee on Employment of People with Disabilities
1331 F Street NW
Suite 300
Washington, DC 20004-1107
Phone: (202) 376-6200

PUBLIC EMPLOYMENT SERVICE

Your state employment service, sometimes called the Job Service, operates in coordination with the Labor Department's U.S. Employment Service. The service has about 1,700 local offices (also called employment service centers) nationwide that help match job seekers with appropriate job openings free of charge. The Job Service also offers counseling and testing to help you choose a career by determining your occupational aptitudes and interests.

JOB COUNSELING SERVICES

The job counseling services offered by your city or town, which can be found in the Yellow Pages of your local phone directory, are another useful option. The

National Board for Certified Counselors will provide you with a listing of certified career counselors in your area. Write:

> National Board for Certified Counselors
> 3D Terrace Way
> Greensboro, NC 27403
> (336) 547-0607

DIRECT CONTACT

One of the best ways to find a job is through the direct contact method. Direct contact means contacting potential employers directly on your own whether they are advertising job openings or not. This method of finding a job will be discussed in detail in Chapter 3.

NETWORKING

Another excellent method to finding a job, and one that I recommend highly, is networking. I'm sure you already understand this concept whether you recognize the term or not. Simply put, it means using contacts that you have to help you get a job. This is a great approach to use even if you don't have any *professional* contacts. Networking takes many forms; with a little skill and some effort, it can be a very productive tool for you. This is such a good way to find a job that it has its own chapter (Chapter 4).

FOR STUDENTS
On-Campus Recruiters

Many college students and their parents assume that they can focus their job-hunting plans solely on those companies that recruit on campus. Approaching a job search campaign in this way is a bad idea; there simply aren't enough companies recruiting on college campuses to provide an ample source of jobs for interested students. Those companies that do recruit on campus typically visit a large number of colleges and receive many more job inquiries than they are able to interview people for, let alone hire people for. It is not uncommon for firms to receive as many as 300 applications for every job opening. The competition is so fierce that a typical student's chances of actually getting a job through the on-campus recruitment process are comparable to the chances of winning a state lottery. It's certainly not *impossible*, but it's very tough.

Nevertheless, it is true that some of the very best positions for college students are offered by companies that recruit on campus. The starting positions at these companies might not seem that much better than jobs you could find by using other job-search methods, but many of these companies offer fast-track training programs; the management training programs in particular offer terrific opportunities. If you decide to pursue on-campus recruiting opportunities, however, make sure that you don't spend all of your time and effort in this area.

One of the most overlooked avenues for jobs is companies that don't actually visit college campuses but do post notices that they are interested in receiving applications from candidates. Many companies try to cut their overhead costs by limiting or eliminating recruiting visits, but they are still interested in hiring people. These companies are not as easily visible to college students as the firms that actually visit campuses, but they can be an even better source of job possibilities due to decreased competition for job openings.

Again, remember that with any of these methods, what doesn't work for other people may actually work for you. Although finding a job through on-campus recruiters can be tough, my brother did it. He got several interviews and landed a great job at a company that told him they don't usually hire people straight out of college.

Why did they do this? One of the keys was that my brother is excellent at interviews and he knows how to job hunt. By the time you're done with this book, you will be, too.

Internships

I think internships are a great way to get a job. Off the top of my head I can think of at least four friends who have gotten good jobs through internships. If you still have a while before graduation, I highly recommend you find an internship in a field you're interested in.

Internships are excellent stepping stones that can lead directly to job opportunities. If a company needs to fill an entry-level position, it will most likely consider its intern before any outside applicants because the intern is already familiar with the company and how it operates, and the company already knows whether the intern would be a good hire, based on previous work.

There are other reasons you should consider an internship. If you aren't sure about what you want to do after graduation, an internship will give you a good idea of what it would be like to work in a particular field. Interns usually get the most tedious work the company has to offer with only glimpses at the more "glorious" work. If you finish your internship finding that the grunt work was no big deal, you'll probably enjoy working in that field.

Internships also strengthen your resume and can provide you with some valuable business contacts. You can then use these contacts in your networking efforts, described above and in Chapter 4.

Career Planning and Placement Offices

Every college and most high schools have either a job placement office or counselors that can steer you in the right direction. Your placement office can help you find a job by matching your qualifications with appropriate job openings. You can also get counseling, testing, and job search advice, and you can take advantage of the school's career resource library. Your college placement office can help you identify and evaluate your interests, work values, and skills. They offer workshops on such topics as job search strategy, resume writing, letter writing, and effective interviewing or job fairs for meeting prospective employers.

Think of your job search as a military campaign; you have to follow every avenue possible to win, but some avenues are likely to be more productive than others. It's hard to say which avenue is going to pan out for you, so you shouldn't rule out any possibilities. At the same time, however, you can't afford to spend too much time in any area that is unlikely to be productive.

You're going to find that after a while you will get a sense of which methods are working for you and which aren't. Once you get a feeling for which methods are producing the best results, shift more of your effort into that area. For example, if you're finding that you're getting lots of phone calls back from the ads you've responded to and none from an employment agency you've asked to help you, focus on the ads.

CHAPTER THREE

Contacting Companies on Your Own

MASS MAILINGS AND PHONE CALLS

Contacting companies on your own does not mean sending out mass mailings or making a barrage of hurried phone calls. Direct contact means making a professional, personal approach to a select group of companies. You need to focus on a particular field or a particular job function for your job search to be effective, and nowhere is that more true than in contacting potential employers directly.

WHAT KINDS OF COMPANIES SHOULD YOU CONTACT?

For starters, can you think of any places that you want to work? Have you heard good things about a company? Add them to your list. Then move on to researching other companies that you might not have thought of or heard of, for that matter.

Aren't the largest, most successful companies the best places to look for a job? Don't they offer the most security? Contrary to what many believe, this is not always the case. In recent years, some of the largest and most successful companies in America have been dramatically downsizing their work force. Should you avoid these companies altogether? No, I'm just saying these companies are not necessarily the most secure places to work. Furthermore, these giants are the very companies that are deluged with resumes and job applications. For example, some of the largest banking corporations receive as many as 3,000 resumes every day!

There are many more moderate-size companies—those with only several hundred employees that are not well known to the general public—that you should contact. These companies are a much better source of jobs: they are large enough to have a number of job openings at any given time, but they are small enough that they are often overlooked by other job hunters. This means that there will be less competition for openings and a greater chance that you will find a job at a company of this size.

The best source of job opportunities are often small companies, especially those with under fifty employees. These companies are not very visible and although there will be fewer job openings per company than at larger firms, there will also be much less competition. Another significant advantage of working for a small firm is that there will probably be significant room for career growth there. At the same time, however, smaller companies are typically less stable than larger firms and offer less job security and fewer benefits. Nevertheless, most job openings today exist within these small companies, and these are the opportunities that are most often overlooked.

Two of the advantages of working for a small company are that you will more likely have a greater range of duties and you will probably have a greater chance of moving up in the company. Greater responsibility often means greater pay. (Often, but not always!)

SOURCES OF COMPANY INFORMATION

So how do you find out which companies you should contact? Well, as discussed earlier, you should know which fields you are most interested in. Do some research and put together a list of the companies in these fields. You should research a number of companies. If you just focus on one company at a time you will soon become very frustrated. Helpful hint: rather than going into great detail in your search at this point, you should get a little bit of information about many different companies.

Where should you go to get this information? The first place is your networking contacts. Take a few minutes to talk with them to see if they work at a place where you would feel comfortable.

Another good source is the *JobBank* series, a group of employment directories listing almost all companies with fifty or more employees in most of the larger cities and metropolitan areas in the United States. Each *JobBank* is a complete research tool for job hunters, providing updated information including:

- The full name, address, and telephone number of each company
- Web sites and e-mail addresses
- Contact name for professional hiring
- Listings of common positions, educational backgrounds sought, and fringe benefits offered
- A section on the region's economic outlook
- The addresses of professional associations, chambers of commerce, and executive search and job placement agencies

The series covers thirty-six different industries, from Accounting to Utilities. The number of employers listed in each book ranges from a few thousand for smaller cities to almost 8,000 for metro New York and Los Angeles. These books are available for the following regions: Atlanta, Austin/San Antonio, Boston, the Carolinas, Chicago, Connecticut, Dallas–Fort Worth, Denver, Detroit, Florida, Houston, Indiana, Las Vegas, Los Angeles, Minneapolis–St. Paul, Missouri, New Mexico, New York City, Northern New England, Ohio, Philadelphia, Phoenix, Pittsburgh, Portland, Salt Lake City, San Francisco, Seattle, Tennessee, Upstate New York, Virginia, Washington D.C., and Wisconsin.

There are other resources you can use to find listings of companies. For example, there are many directories available, such as *Dun & Bradstreet's Million Dollar Directory* and *Standard & Poor's* investment guide, that list basic information about companies, such as the name of the president and a brief description of the company's products and/or services. These directories, as well as many state manufacturer listings, can be found in your local library. The advantage that the *JobBank* series has over these directories is that they list typical entry-level positions for each firm and include the name of the person you should contact.

One of my favorite methods for getting information is looking at a company's Web site. You can find company Web sites listed in books like the *JobBank* series, you can search the Web using a search engine, or you can look in the classifieds. Companies will often include their Web site address in their classified ad.

Once I get the address, I do most of my research from the company's Web site. They often include company history, product information, sales information, information on the work environment, and more. You then use this information to write a targeted, informed cover letter.

A hiring manager would much rather read a letter with phrases like, "I would love to work for Spacely Sprockets because I know you're the number one producer of widgets," rather than "I would love to work for your company." The first sentence shows that you did your research. (I'll discuss more about cover letters in Chapter 9.)

This type of information also comes in handy during the interview. Hiring managers often ask questions like, "Tell me why you want to work here," "What do you like most about our company," and more.

When researching companies, remember that your aim at this point is to learn a little bit about many companies. You do not need a tremendous amount of information before you contact a firm, particularly if you're up to speed with what's going on in the industry.

THE BEST WAY TO CONTACT SMALL AND LARGE COMPANIES

How you go about contacting a company depends upon the size of the firm. At small firms, such as those with under fifty employees, you should contact the president directly. There's a good chance that the president of the company himself or herself will be highly involved in the recruitment process. If not, that person will pass your resume on to the proper hiring manager.

As a general rule, you should always try to contact a department head or the president of a company—even for moderate-size companies with several hundred employees and large companies with over 1,000 employees. But as you apply to larger and larger companies, you will find yourself more and more often bumped back to the personnel office.

Do not let this discourage you. The personnel office is where a great deal of hiring is done; it can be a very valuable resource. There are many books on the market that tell you to avoid personnel offices because it's their job to weed out the candidates. Sometimes there is no way around it however. Some presidents and hiring managers will send every resume they receive to human resources, whether it's a good candidate or a bad one. As soon as they see a resume, they send it off.

The first step you should take in contacting a company directly is sending out your resume with a cover letter. The letter should be addressed to a specific person; try to avoid sending letters to "To whom it may concern," "To the Personnel Office," etc. I usually tell people to send it to the department head. If for example you're applying as an entry-level accountant, find out who the head of accounting is or who the hiring manager in that department is. You can usually get this information by calling the company, looking at company information literature, consulting sources like the *JobBank* series, or going on the Web.

After you have sent your letter and allowed sufficient time for the person to receive it, you should call. The idea is to call that person one or two days after your resume arrives so that you will be more likely to be remembered.

Can you call the company to see if there are any job openings *before* you make the effort of sending your resume? If you are unusually confident and articulate on the phone, you may have success with this approach. Such calls are especially effective if you are contacting smaller companies since you are more likely to reach a key decision-maker directly, rather than being blocked by a secretary. However, at larger companies you will find that simply sending a resume and cover letter is a much more effective method.

FOLLOWING UP WITH A PHONE CALL

After you've sent your resume and cover letter, you should always follow up with a phone call. What you should say on the phone is important, but so is how you say it. You need to speak with confidence; even though there may not be a job opening available at a certain company, you shouldn't be apologetic for making a call. All companies hire at some point, and each has, at least in theory, a responsibility to be courteous when an outsider makes a call inquiring about potential job openings.

Will all of your calls be answered courteously? No. Some will be answered very abruptly; often you'll be calling somebody who is very busy. But you must project confidence on the phone. Remember, one of the most important things that companies are looking for in entry-level hires is maturity and confidence. One of the ways you can express these qualities is by sounding confident on the phone.

It is extremely important that you be succinct and to the point on the phone. One good way to do this is by writing out a short script for yourself before you call. You should be sure not to sound as if you're reading this script, but do become very familiar with it so you won't forget what you want to say even if you're nervous. You need to make three points:

1. Why you are calling
2. Why you would be a strong candidate for hiring
3. What kind of position you're interested in

You should do this very briefly, in twenty seconds or less. At the same time, however, you must be sure to speak clearly and slowly enough to be understood. You should also remember that not all of your calls are going to be well received. And I highly recommend that you don't keep calling over and over and make a pest of yourself. The point is to call once so your name sticks out in the hiring manager's mind.

What Should a Follow-Up Phone Call Sound Like?

Let's say you're calling a very small bank, perhaps a bank that has one office and employs thirty people. Because the bank is so small, you should try to speak with the president. Here is an example:

| Receptionist: | *Good morning, Main Street Bank. Can I help you?* |
| You: | *Good morning! I'd like to speak with Mr. Smith, please.* |

For this example, Mr. Smith is the president of the bank. Your call is then transferred to his office.

| Secretary: | *Mr. Smith's office.* |
| You: | *Good Morning! This is William McNeill calling. Is Mr. Smith available?* |

I suggest that you don't tell the secretary at this point that you are calling about a job, because the secretary might then block your call. Instead, you want to sound professional and businesslike, as if there is a good reason why you are calling Mr. Smith—which there is. However, if you are asked why you would like to speak to Mr. Smith, you will have to try to sell the secretary on the idea of you working for that firm, just as if you were talking to Mr. Smith.

Secretary:	*Mr. Smith is very busy. Can I tell him what this is regarding?*
You:	*Yes, my name is William McNeill. I just graduated with honors from City University with a degree in Finance. I am seeking an entry-level position at your bank as a loan officer.*
Secretary:	*We don't have any openings at this point in time.*
You:	*Well, that's fine. I understand that might be the case. But I would like to have a couple of minutes to speak with Mr. Smith anyway, in case something might come up in the future. I know he's very busy; I only need to speak with him for a moment.*

With a little luck, the secretary will then put your call through to Mr. Smith. It is very important that you try to speak with Mr. Smith even if you are told that there aren't any jobs available. If you do and if a job opportunity arises in a couple of months, you might have a chance to interview for the position before it is advertised. Don't take "no openings at this time" to mean "no openings ever"—it doesn't!

Be polite but aggressive in your job search. Show that you are genuinely interested in the firm. If you are talking to a department head or the president of the company, that person may be in a position to create a job for you.

If your call gets rerouted through personnel, try to use this same strategy. Get the decision-maker on the phone, briefly explain why you're calling, demonstrate that you're a strong candidate for hiring, and request an interview. If you are successful in getting Mr. Smith (or any decision-maker) on the phone, the conversation might go like this:

Mr. Smith:	*Hello?*
You:	*Hi! Is this Mr. Smith?*
Mr. Smith:	*Yes, this is he.*
You:	*Mr. Smith, my name is William McNeill and I've just graduated from City University with a degree in Finance, and I very much want to pursue a career in banking. I'm interested in becoming a loan officer and I know that you may not have any openings at this time, but I would like to come by and talk to you for a couple of minutes about the opportunities that might be available in banking. I sent you a resume and cover letter last week. Did you receive my letter?*

One of the reasons you want to ask if Mr. Smith has received your letter is because you're trying to get a conversation started. Mr. Smith might respond by saying, "Yes, I read your letter, I saw that you've done such and such…" If he does not recall your letter, briefly summarize its contents.

Avoid saying something like, "Mr. Smith, do you have a job there now?" It's very easy for Mr. Smith to say no and end the conversation. Instead ask if he's received your letter, get a polite, upbeat conversation started, and request an interview. What if the call doesn't go so smoothly? Here is an example of one way to handle tougher calls:

Mr. Smith:	*Hello?*
You:	*Mr. Smith?*
Mr. Smith:	*Yes, this is he.*
You:	*Mr. Smith, my name is William McNeill. I've just graduated from City College.*
Mr. Smith:	*Will, I got your letter, and I want to thank you for thinking of our bank. I think you have some very strong credentials, and I'm sure you're going to do very well, but we don't have any job openings at the moment.*
You:	*I understand that you might not have any job openings right now. I've lived in this area for a while, and as I've indicated, I very much want to pursue a career in banking here. I'd like to have a chance to meet with you just for a couple of minutes anyway, just to see if you could tell me a little bit about the banking industry in this town and a little bit about the opportunities one might expect at those places that might be hiring. Would this be possible?*

This way, you're showing Mr. Smith some important things: You're a confident, professional individual; you're courteous; you're *not* demanding a job, but you would like to have the opportunity to talk with him briefly. If he says yes, great, if he says no, thank him for his time and move on.

I want to mention again that whatever you do, don't call repeatedly and pester the hiring manager. Believe me when I say they will most likely remember you after one or two calls. Even if they don't, it's better than pestering them and having them filing your resume in the circular file. As a person who receives a lot of these calls, I can tell you that I don't mind if a person calls once or twice. But if the person calls me every four days for a month, they start to annoy me, and they just kill their chances of ever getting hired.

CHAPTER FOUR

Networking Your Way to the Top

Networking is the process of exchanging information, contacts, and experience for professional purposes. One reason so many people use networking is that it's a great method for finding a new or better job.

DEVELOPING YOUR CONTACTS

Some career counselors feel that the best route to a better job is through somebody you already know or to whom you can be introduced. These counselors recommend that you build your contact base beyond your current acquaintances by asking each one to introduce you, or refer you, to additional people in your field of interest.

The theory goes like this: You might start with fifteen personal contacts, each of whom introduces you to three additional people, for a total of forty-five additional contacts. Then each of these people introduces you to three other people, which adds one hundred thirty-five contacts. Theoretically, you'll soon know every person in the industry.

Of course, developing your personal contacts doesn't work quite as smoothly as the theory suggests, because some people won't be able to introduce you to anyone. The further you stray from your initial contact base, the weaker your references may be. So, if you do try developing your own contacts, begin with as many people whom you know personally as you can. Dig into your personal phone book and your holiday greeting card list and locate old classmates from school. Be sure to approach people who perform your personal business, like your lawyer, accountant, banker, doctor, stockbroker, and insurance agent. By the nature of their professions, these people develop a broad contact base.

By Mail

It's essential to achieve the right tone in your networking letters. Unless you're familiar with a contact, word your correspondence in a businesslike manner. In other words, don't use your addressee's first name or an overly casual writing style. Likewise, if you've been in contact with this person recently, it could be useful to remind him or her, "It was great seeing you at the Chicago Writers' Convention last month" or "It's been several months since we bumped into each other on that flight to London. How are you?"

Many networking letters are written to an addressee to whom the candidate has been referred to by a mutual acquaintance. In this case, immediately state the name of the person who referred you, such as "Jean Rawlins suggested I contact you." It is generally more effective to ask a contact with whom you are unfamiliar for assistance and names of people to contact than to ask for a job. Chances are, if your letter is politely persuasive, people will be interested in talking with you.

By Phone

A good self-introduction is a tremendous asset to your networking agenda. Aim for a balance of brevity and completeness. Don't simply call someone and say, "Hi, Mr. Pitt. This is George. Elaine told me you do quite a business in the stock market. Do you mind telling me about it?" Write out a short statement, including not only what you want but also who you are and how you're qualified. If you waste people's time, their opinion of you will take a nosedive. So practice your delivery before giving the pitch, and make sure to tailor each one to the situation at hand.

Many people are, at first, a little uncomfortable calling people they don't know and asking for contact names and interviews. You'll be nervous the first few times, but with practice you'll feel much more comfortable and confident making calls. The key is to think about what you're going to say in advance, pick up that phone, and just do it. No one else can network for you. Once you gain some confidence, you'll find that your calls will make a big difference in your job-search campaign.

Networking Wherever You Are

Networking is a commitment. Always be on the lookout for new opportunities. You never know when or where you'll meet your new employer or an industry expert. Being prepared to network in even the oddest settings will have you interviewing for more positions than you ever thought possible.

SEND A THANK-YOU LETTER

If a networking contact has been particularly helpful to you, by all means send a thank-you note. Not only is this courteous, it keeps your contacts current. That person may be an important business contact for years to come—especially if the individual is active in your industry.

FOR STUDENTS AND RECENT GRADUATES

Traditionally, networking is used by people with a great deal of work experience. But you can use it even if you have no experience whatsoever. Perhaps you're asking yourself, "Don't I have to know people who are in a position to hire to be able to network? Don't I have to know a lot of people in general, or in a specific geographic area, to get a job through networking?" The answer to both questions is no. You don't have to know anybody at all; *you just have to get to know people.*

THE KEY TO NETWORKING

One of the secrets of networking is knowing what you want—or at least appearing to know what you want. If, when you are making networking calls, you tell your contacts you're interested in the industry they work in and if you sound even somewhat knowledgeable about that industry, that makes you more or less an industry insider.

How do you start? Keep up to date with the industry. Read the trade publications. These are specialized journals and magazines that address the concerns of professionals in a given industry. Virtually every type of business has at least one.

COME PREPARED

Your friends may not have any close relations with professionals, but their parents might. Asking close pals to contact their relatives on your behalf is a most effective way of building a network—as long as you have no problem reciprocating the favor. Teachers come into contact with experts from various fields on a daily basis. Asking them about their associates may secure you several informational interviews with leaders in each industry.

ALUMNI PLACEMENT OFFICES

These services are now part of many universities and colleges. They function basically as clearinghouses for interested companies in attempting to match job-seeking alumni to their needs. If your school doesn't offer placement services, try to take advantage of the membership listings many alumni associations make available, which can serve as a valuable source for contacts.

NAME DROPPING

Be sure to drop names; it's one of the most important ways to get ahead in the business world. ("Sally Kendrick suggested I call you.") As you continue networking, you'll find yourself dropping names of people you've met only by phone. If you're uncomfortable with this, you shouldn't be; this is the way it's done. Someday you may be in a position to help other job seekers this way, but right now, you need to do everything you can to increase your chances of finding a job.

WHAT DOES A NETWORKING CONVERSATION SOUND LIKE?

Here's a sample of what your networking conversations should sound like:

> You: *Hi, Uncle Ted! It's Emily. As you might have heard, I just graduated from college, and I want to pursue a career in banking. Is there anyone you can think of who might be willing to talk to me about the banking industry, to fill me in on some background information?*
>
> Uncle Ted: *I really can't think of anyone in the banking industry, but why don't you call up my attorney, Don Silva. He's not a real close friend, but I deal with him every month or so. He knows a lot of businesspeople, not necessarily in the banking industry, but you never know. Why don't you call him and see if he can be of any help. His number is 555-1212.*
>
> You: *Thanks, Uncle Ted!*

You then call the attorney, immediately identifying who referred you:

> You: *Mr. Silva, my name is Emily Sampson. My uncle, Ted Larson, suggested I call you. I'm interested in a career in banking, and I wondered if you might know anyone in that field who might be able to talk to me briefly about the industry.*
>
> Attorney: *Well, I'm not really sure. Let me think about it a little, and I'll get back to you.*

Keep the momentum on your side by offering to follow up yourself.

> You: *That's great. Why don't you think about it for a couple of days, and I'll call you back. If there's someone in the industry you can refer me to or someone who might know somebody else in the industry, I'd really appreciate it.*

If a networking contact seems reluctant, you could redirect the conversation in this way:

Attorney: *Gee, I do know a few people in the industry, but they're probably not hiring now....*

You: *That's fine. I just want to talk to someone briefly to find out what's going on in the industry. If you'd like, I can stop by for a few minutes at your convenience so we can meet, and in the meantime maybe you could think of some other names you'd feel comfortable referring me to.*

That way, if your contact is hesitant to give any names out without seeing in person that you're a polished, professional individual, you may be able to overcome some of that reluctance by setting up a face-to-face meeting. This technique also gives your contact the opportunity to think of some more names of people he can refer you to.

The attorney example is a good one; you should consider meeting with people who service others in your chosen industry. If the contact is still unwilling to meet with you, don't be overly insistent. Instead, ask the contact to recommend someone else for you to call. Eventually, you should network your way to someone who works within your chosen industry.

DON'T ASK FOR A JOB

Remember, you don't want to scare your contacts off. If for some reason you suspect a particular contact is in a position to hire, you should not specifically ask about a job. Ask about the industry, relay that you are interested in pursuing a career in that field, and try to set up a time to meet briefly so you can get some background information.

Suppose you know for a fact that a certain contact has an opening available for which you'd be suitable. Perhaps you saw the ad in the classifieds. Should you mention it in your conversation with this person? Absolutely not. Remember, you earned this contact through networking, not by reading a classified ad. (Of course, if the person asks whether you saw the ad, don't lie, but point out that you're calling as a result of speaking to so-and-so.) You want to position yourself as an industry insider who is networking around, not as just another person responding to an ad.

CHAPTER FIVE

Important Resume Basics

This chapter will go over all the background information you'll need to know before you start with actually writing your resume. Even if you already know something about resumes, I recommend that you still read this chapter. Even if you only pick up one tip, it will be well worth it. Also, the general consensus on how to write a resume has changed. You don't want to be using old methods that will scream "outdated" to a potential employer. This book incorporates all the latest information.

When filling a position, an employer will often have over a hundred applicants but time to interview only a handful of the most promising ones. As a result, a recruiter will reject most applicants after only briefly skimming their resumes.

Unless you've phoned and talked to the employer, which you should do whenever you can, you'll be chosen or rejected entirely on the basis of your resume and cover letter. *Your cover letter must catch the employer's attention, and your resume must hold it.* The two most important aspects of your resume are the appearance and the content.

FORMAT

First impressions matter, so make sure the recruiter's first impression of your resume is a good one. The most common resume formats are the chronological resume and the functional resume. You may also see references to a "chrono-functional," or "combination," resume, but this is usually a variant on one of the other two—a chronological type with an expanded skills summary or a functional type with an expanded work history section. Although I'll discuss all types, the examples you will see in this book will for the most part follow a simple, chronological format.

Chronological

The chronological format is the most common. Choose a chronological format if you're currently working or were working recently and if your most recent experiences relate to your desired field. To a recruiter, the last job you held (or still have) and your latest schooling are the most important, so put the last first and list the rest going back in time. In other words, you'll be listing your experience in reverse chronological order, starting with your most recent job.

Functional

A functional resume focuses on skills and strengths, while de-emphasizing job titles, employers, etc. In other words, instead of concentrating on listing individual jobs in order, you would group all relevant skills together. A functional resume may be useful if you have no work experience, have been out of the work force for a long time, or are changing careers, but some recruiters may wonder if you're trying to hide something, so be ready for questions of that nature. Some professional resume writers actually recommend sticking with a chronological resume at all costs. The examples throughout this book follow the chronological format because it's the most widely accepted and it will be the easiest for you to start with.

TYPING

Use a word processing program to generate your resume. If you don't own a computer, you can either use a friend's, go to a printing store like Kinko's that allows you to use computers for a small hourly fee, or try your state employment service.

A word processing program like Word or WordPerfect allows you the flexibility to make changes instantly and store different drafts. Choose a basic font like Times New Roman for your resume. Also, use either 10-point or 12-point type (this is the size of the actual letters) for your resume. Many other options are also available, like boldface or italics for emphasis and the ability to manipulate spacing. Do not justify the right side of your resume.

Organization

Your name, phone number, e-mail address (if you have one), and mailing address should be at the top of the resume. Make your name stand out by using a slightly larger font size and boldface. Be sure to spell out everything; don't abbreviate "St." for "Street" or "Rd." for "Road." The word "present" (as in "1997– present") should be lowercase.

Next, list your experience, then your education. If you're a recent graduate or student, list your education first, unless your experience is more important than your education. (For example, if you've just graduated from a teaching school, have some business experience, and are applying for a job in business, list your business experience first.)

The important thing is to break up the text in some logical way that makes your resume visually attractive and easy to scan, so experiment to see which layout works best. However you set it up, *stay consistent*. Inconsistencies in fonts, spacing, or tenses make your resume look sloppy. Use tabs rather than the less precise space bar to keep information aligned vertically.

I'll go over all these points in much greater detail in the next chapter, so don't worry about writing your information just yet.

Abbreviations

It's advisable to spell out most abbreviations on a resume. Resumes are compressed enough as it is; frequent abbreviations and acronyms can make them nearly unintelligible.

Length

Employers dislike long resumes, so keep it to one page. If you must squeeze in more information than would otherwise fit, try using a slightly smaller typeface or changing the margins. Watch also for "widows" (a word or two on a separate line at the end of a paragraph). You can often free up some space if you can shorten the information enough to get rid of those single words taking up an entire line. Another tactic that works with some word processing programs is to decrease the size of your paragraph returns and change the spacing between lines.

PAPER

Use standard 8 1/2-by-11-inch paper. A smaller size will appear more personal than professional and is easily lost in an employer's files; a larger size will look awkward and may be discarded for not fitting with other documents.

Use quality paper that has weight and texture, in a conservative color like white or ivory. Good resume paper is easy to find at stores that sell stationery or office products and is even available at some drug stores. Use matching paper for your resume and cover letter and matching envelopes to go with them. One hiring manager at a major magazine throws out all resumes that arrive on paper that differs in color from the envelope! I think this is a little nitpicky, but why take the chance?

Do not buy paper with images of clouds and rainbows in the background or anything that looks like casual stationery you would send your favorite aunt. Do not spray perfume or cologne on your resume. Also, never use the stationery of your current employer.

PRINTING

Use a laser printer when possible. Quality ink-jet and bubble-jet printers are usually okay, but make sure you choose the "best" or "high" printing option in your word processing program. Likewise, if you're only printing out a rough copy you can use the "draft" option for printing to save time and ink. Do not use a dot matrix printer. Print out each copy individually. I do not recommend using a photocopier because many photocopiers have imperfections that will show. Also, remember your final resume should be on resume paper anyway. Household typewriters and office typewriters are no longer a good option.

Watermark Position

When you print your resume (and cover letter), hold it up to the light to make sure the watermark reads correctly—that it's not upside-down or backward. As trivial as this may sound, it's the accepted style in formal correspondence, and some recruiters check for it. One recruiter at a law firm in New Hampshire sheepishly admitted this is the first thing he checks: "I open each envelope and check the watermarks on the resume and cover letter. Those resumes that have it wrong go into a different pile."

PROOFREAD WITH CARE

Mistakes on resumes are not only embarrassing, but they will often remove you from consideration (particularly if something obvious, like your name, is misspelled). No matter how much you paid someone else to type or write your resume, you're the one who loses if there is a mistake. So proofread it as carefully as possible. Get a friend to help you. Read your draft aloud as your friend checks the proof copy. Then have your friend read aloud while you check. Next, read it letter by letter to check spelling and punctuation.

You should see the reaction on people's faces when I'm interviewing them and I tell them I found a mistake on their resume. Some people get totally flustered. Some people handle it really well. How they react to this one situation alone can make or break an entire interview. Why put yourself in that situation if you don't have to? Make sure there are no mistakes.

If you're having your resume typed by a resume service or a printer and you don't have time to proof it, pay for it and take it home. Proof it there and bring it back later to get it corrected and printed.

If you wrote your resume with a word processing program, use the built-in spell checker to double-check for spelling errors. Keep in mind that a spell checker will not find errors like "to" for "two" or "wok" for "work." Many spell-check programs don't recognize missing or misused punctuation, nor are they set to check the spelling of capitalized words. It's important to still proofread your resume for grammatical mistakes and other problems, even after it's been spell-checked.

If you find mistakes, do not fix them with pen, pencil, or correction fluid! Make the changes on the computer and print out the resume again.

CONTENT

You're selling your skills and accomplishments in your resume, so it's important to inventory yourself and know yourself. If you've achieved something, say so. Put it in the best possible light. But avoid subjective statements, like "I am a hard worker" or "I get along well with my coworkers." Stick to the facts.

While you shouldn't hold back or be modest, don't exaggerate your achievements to the point of misrepresentation. Be honest. Many companies will immediately drop an applicant from consideration (or fire a current employee) upon discovering inaccurate or untrue information on a resume or other application material.

Write down the important (and pertinent) things you've done, but do it in as few words as possible. Short, concise phrases are more effective than longwinded sentences. Avoid the use of "I" when emphasizing your accomplishments. Instead, use phrases beginning with action verbs. Use present tense for your current job and past tense for previous jobs.

Also, try to hold your paragraphs to six lines or less. If you have more than six lines of information about one job or school, put it in two or more paragraphs. A short resume will be examined more carefully. Remember: your resume usually has between eight and forty-five seconds to catch an employer's eye, so make every second count.

Give 'Em What They Want

Employers favor certain skills. Here are the top contenders:

- Supervising/managing skills mean you can take responsibility for the work of others.
- Coordinating/organizing skills allow you to plan events or see projects to completion.
- Negotiating skills allow you to bring about compromise and resolve differences.
- Customer service/public relations skills enable you to be a spokesperson for your organization.
- Training/instructing skills allow you to show newcomers the ropes.

- Interviewing skills enable you to ask tough questions, then listen to get insight from the answers.
- Speaking skills involve presenting your ideas verbally in a coherent fashion.
- Writing skills enable you to express your ideas convincingly on paper.
- Deadline-meeting skills enable you to work under pressure.
- Budgeting skills involve the ability to save your employer money.

Avoid Catchphrases

In the course of a job search, it's tempting to use catchphrases you've picked up from advertisements or reference materials, phrases that sound as though they should go in a resume or cover letter. Many people are tempted to reach for expressions like "self-starter," "excellent interpersonal skills," and "work well independently or as part of a team." These are all overused expressions, and, in most cases, obvious. Who would ever write, "I'm a lone nut who hates working on teams"?

Improve on these descriptions by listing actual projects and goals. For example, change "Determined achiever with proven leadership skills" to "Supervised staff of fifteen and increased the number of projects completed before deadline by ten percent." In other words, list specifics. Once you begin working, employers will discover your personal attributes for themselves. While you're under consideration, concrete experiences are more valuable than vague phrases or obscure promises.

Objectives and Summaries

The original objective of the objective was to identify what type of position you were looking for and what you hoped to get out of it. At first I was a huge fan of objectives. I liked summing up what I wanted in one sentence. I loved the fact that I could clearly and succinctly convey what job I was looking for.

Now I don't like objectives as much. After thinking about this issue, I've decided that I'm no longer going to recommend putting an objective on a resume. There are four main reasons why I say this.

If you want to identify what job you're interested in, use the first paragraph of your cover letter. Here are some quick examples: I'm applying for the position of Welder that I saw advertised in this Sunday's *Globe*, or I'm applying for an entry-level position in your department. (There will be more on cover letters later in the book.)

The second reason is that several human resource reps told me that they sometimes use the objective to eliminate a candidate. If for example, the open position is for an entry-level accountant, people who say they're looking for an accounting position with supervisory duties have been eliminated from the running.

A third reason is that, over the years, job objectives have become overused and generic. Have you ever used this one before? *I am a detail-oriented team player looking for a position where I can continue to grow and apply my skills.* Well, so has everyone else in the world. Plus, it states the obvious. Who in their right mind would ever write: *I am a lazy person who overlooks the obvious in search of a position where I can continue to get by on the minimum amount of effort required?*

The fourth reason I am no longer a big fan of job objectives is that I found a new fascination—the summary. I like using summaries because I can use a couple of sentences to highlight key skills or awards that may not normally fit into the normal flow of an outline or cover letter. But beware of running the risk of turning a summary into an even longer and more boring and generic job objective. A lot of times you can find another home for the information you want to put into a summary in either the cover letter or later in the resume. Many of my resume-writing colleagues don't use summaries.

So what do I recommend for you, the first-time resume writer? Don't bother with a job objective or a summary. Just start right in with the meat of the resume. If you're a new graduate or you want to highlight your academic achievements, start with the education section (more on this later). If you have good job experience, start with that (again, more on this later).

In summary, I would not use a job objective and would only use a summary if you're fairly sure it's unique and interesting. Otherwise, use your cover letter to state which job you are applying for, and start your resume off with the actual information.

There are certain instances, however, when an objective may be suitable, for example, if your previous work experience is unrelated to the position for which you're applying, or if you're a recent graduate with no work experience. Sometimes an objective can give a functional resume focus. One or two sentences describing the job you're seeking may clarify the capacity in which your skills can best be put to use. Be sure your objective is in line with the position for which you're applying, and don't state that you're looking for a position that will allow you to grow or to develop certain capacities. Employers are interested in what you can do for them, not what they can do for you. This is something to keep in mind throughout the job-search and interview process. Ask not what the company can do for you, but what you can do for the company.

Experience

Emphasize continued experience in a particular job area or continued interest in a particular industry. De-emphasize irrelevant positions. Delete positions you held for less than four months (unless you're a recent college graduate or still in school). It's okay to include one opening line providing a general description of each company at which you've worked.

Stress your results and achievements, elaborating on how you contributed in your previous jobs. Did you increase sales, reduce costs, improve a product, implement a new program? Were you promoted? Use specific numbers (quantities, percentages, dollar amounts) whenever possible.

Gaps in Your Employment History

You may be asked about gaps in your employment history. Although you'll need to be prepared to explain them, gaps aren't the stigma they used to be. Many people now have some kind of irregularity in their work histories; they were laid off, went back to school, took time off for personal reasons, changed careers, had a baby—you name it. Because this is now so prevalent, recruiters can't very well hold it against you, as long as you have a plausible explanation and the skills for the job.

Action Verbs

In describing previous work experiences, the strongest resumes use short phrases beginning with action verbs. Remember, however, that if you upload your resume to an online job-hunting Web site like CareerCity, the keywords or key nouns a computer would search for become as important as action verbs. (More on this in Chapter 8.)

Bullets

Bullets are useful for drawing attention to significant points, but a resume can be too bullety. A long column of bullet points in random order often lacks coherence and can be as much of a deterrent as long paragraphs. An alternative is to group them conceptually, in relevant categories, with a few bullets under each one, to make them easier to grasp. This may also permit you to combine several bullets into one or, conversely, to break up long paragraphs.

Avoid Excessive Jargon

Some technical terms may be necessary, but try to avoid excessive jargon Keep in mind that the first person to see your resume may be a human resources person who won't necessarily know all the jargon and can't be impressed by something he or she doesn't understand.

Skills

Most jobs now require computer knowledge. Therefore, it's usually advisable to include a section titled "Computer Skills," in which you list software programs you know. If the list is long, subdivide them by category.

Computer Skills

Operating systems	**DOS, Windows, Macintosh**
Writing/publishing tools	**Word, WordPerfect, QuarkXPress, PageMaker, Photoshop, Illustrator**
Business (or financial) tools	**Excel, Lotus 1-2-3, Access**
Languages	**C++, BASIC**

It isn't necessary to include the version number of an application. Nor do you need to be perfectly fluent with a program to list it. As long as you've used it in the past and could pick it up again with a little practice, it's legitimate to include it.

The skills section is also an ideal place to mention fluency in a foreign language. If you're listing skills other than computer knowledge, subdivide them by category under the "Skills" heading: "Computer," "Foreign Languages," etc.

Education

Keep the education section brief if you have more than two years of career experience. Elaborate more if you have less experience. Of course if you're still a student or are a recent graduate, the education section should be more detailed. If you're a recent college graduate, you may choose to include high school activities that are directly relevant to your career.

Mention any certifications or licenses you hold; mention degrees received and any honors or special awards. Note individual courses that might be relevant to employers. (These should be at least a semester long. Shorter courses of a day or two, even a week or two, should generally not be mentioned unless they're important in your field. It's also unnecessary to list courses taken in pursuit of a degree.)

Personal Information

Don't include your age, health, physical characteristics, marital status, race, religion, political/moral beliefs, or any other personal information. List your personal interests and hobbies only if they're directly relevant to the type of job you're seeking. If you're applying to a company that greatly values teamwork, for instance, citing that you organized a community fundraiser or played on a basketball team may be advantageous. When in doubt, however, leave it out.

Do not include your picture with your resume unless you have a specific and appropriate reason to do so, for example, if you're applying for a job as an actor or model.

Professional Affiliations

It is worth noting if you're a member of a professional organization in your industry (like the Professional Association of Resume Writers).

References

"References available upon request" is unnecessary on a resume. It's understood that if you're considered for the position, you'll be asked for references and will provide them. Don't send references with your resume and cover letter unless they're specifically requested. I would have them ready to go at any time in case you are asked for them over the phone or at an interview.

WHEN TO GET HELP

If you write reasonably well, it's to your advantage to write your own resume. This forces you to review your experiences and to figure out how to explain your accomplishments in clear, brief phrases. This will help you when you explain your work to interviewers. It's also easier to tailor your resume to each position you're applying for when you've put it together yourself.

If you have difficulty writing in resume style (which is quite unlike normal written language), if you're unsure which parts of your background to emphasize, or if you think your resume would make your case better if it didn't follow the standard forms outlined either here or in a book on resumes, consider having it professionally written.

The best way to choose a resume writer is by reputation: the recommendation of a friend, a personnel director, your school placement officer, or someone else knowledgeable in the field.

Important Questions to Ask a Resume Writer

Asking the following questions will help you determine if a resume writer is right for your needs.

"How long have you been writing resumes?"
"If I'm not satisfied with what you write, will you go over it with me and change it?"
"Do you charge by the hour or a flat rate?"

For more information on resume services, contact:

Professional Association of Resume Writers
3637 Fourth Street, Suite 330, St. Petersburg FL 33704.
Attention: Mr. Frank Fox, Executive Director

Price and Quality

There is no sure relation between price and quality, except that you're unlikely to get a good writer for less than $50 for an uncomplicated resume. The top resume writers will charge several hundred dollars for a resume of an executive with a detailed resume. Chances are that your resume will not be this complicated, so don't pay this much. Don't pick a resume writer simply because he or she has the lowest price. This is not a good indicator of what you are going to get for your money. Printing charges will be extra. Don't forget to look it over before the final version is printed out. It's your career at stake if your resume has mistakes!

Few resume services will give you a firm price over the phone, simply because some resumes are too complicated and take too long to do for a predetermined price. Some services will quote you a price that applies to almost all of their customers. Once you decide to use a specific writer, you should insist on a firm price quote before engaging his or her services. Also, find out how expensive minor changes will be.

FOR STUDENTS AND RECENT GRADUATES

Which Type of Resume Is Right For You?

The type of resume you use depends on your job experience. If you don't have any work history, use a functional resume format, emphasizing your strong points:

- Education. This should be your primary focus.
- Special achievements. This could be almost anything from having an article published to graduating with honors.
- Awards and competitive scholarships
- Classes, internships, theses, or special projects that relate to your job objective
- Computer knowledge. Are you familiar with a Mac or PC? What software programs do you know?
- Language skills. Are you fluent in a foreign language? Be sure to indicate both written and verbal skills.
- Volunteer work
- Committees and organizations
- Extracurricular activities

Recruiters like to see some kind of work history, even if it doesn't relate to your job objective, because it demonstrates that you have a good work ethic. However, it's also important to emphasize special skills or qualifications, including the above information.

Work History

When describing your work history, avoid simply listing your job duties. Focus on accomplishments and achievements, even if they're small. Consider the difference:

Weak: *"Lifeguard at busy public beach. Responsible for safety of bathers and cleanliness of the beach and parking areas."*

Strong: *"Lifeguard at busy public beach. Rescued eight people during summer. Established recycling program for bottles and cans."*

If you've held many jobs, you may choose to emphasize only two or three of the most relevant and list the rest under the heading "Other Experience" without individual job descriptions:

Other Experience: *Floor and stockroom clerk at university bookstore; server, lifeguard, and courier.*

When to Use a Functional Format

As indicated earlier, under some circumstances, a functional resume may be more appropriate. These may include the following:

- You haven't worked for over a year.
- You want to highlight specific skills by category that would not stand out as easily with a chronological format.
- You've held a variety of jobs.
- Your career goal has taken a dramatic turn.

In this case, a functional resume may be more suitable. It focuses not so much on what positions you've held and when but on what you've learned from your experiences that would be useful in the job. The functions you served in your old jobs are the crux of this format. The actual titles and dates don't come until the very end.

GPA

Never include a grade point average (GPA) under 3.0 on your resume. If your GPA in your major is higher than your overall GPA, include it either in addition to or instead of your overall GPA.

High School Information

Including high school information is not recommended for people who have been in the working world and have good experience. Listing high school information is optional for college students and recent graduates, but such information should be used sparingly. If you have exceptional achievements in college and in summer or part-time jobs, omit your high school information. High school information should really only be used if the experience is directly related to the types of jobs or industry for which you are applying. If you decide to include high school achievements, describe them more briefly than your college achievements.

Of course, if you're still in high school or have just graduated, then your high school information can be very important, especially if you don't have a lot of work experience. We've discussed some of the ways to handle limited work experience in this chapter, but we'll go into more detail in the next chapter.

Keep in Touch

Put your home address and phone number at the top of the resume. Change the message on your answering machine if necessary; the Beastie Boys blaring in the background or your sorority sisters screaming may not come across well to all recruiters. If you think you may be moving within six months, include a second address and phone number of a trusted friend or relative who can reach you no matter where you are.

Remember that employers may keep your resume on file and contact you months later if a position opens that fits your qualifications. All too often, candidates are unreachable because they moved and didn't provide enough contact options on their resumes.

CHAPTER SIX

How to Assemble Your Resume

This chapter will take you step by step through the resume-writing process. The best way to go about this is to read this chapter through, and then go back through a second time with your pen and paper ready. This way, after you read it once, you'll have some time to think of all the jobs you've had and gather up any information that might help jog your memory.

There are many resume formats to use. I'm going to outline a basic, chronological format that I recommend to first-time resume writers. Remember that some elements of the resume will vary. For example, you may decide to insert a summary of qualifications. I'm going to number the important parts of the resume so you can follow along more easily.

1. Name

Write your name, in capital letters, as you wish it to appear on your resume. Center it horizontally on the page, about one inch from the top. Use your formal name, even if no one ever calls you by it. Use a middle name or initial, if possible; it adds prestige.

Example

STEVEN M. PHILLIPS

I like to use a type size one or two sizes bigger than the rest of the resume. For example, if I'm using 12 point for the body of the resume, I like to use 14 point for my name. Consider using boldface as well.

2. Address/Phone

Your address and phone number should appear below your name, centered in the middle of the page as well. Don't use abbreviations like St. for Street or Ave. for Avenue. You may, however, use the common abbreviation for your state.

STEVEN M. PHILLIPS
507 North 6th Street
Houston, TX 77024
713/555-1234

If you're a college student, place your school address at the left-hand margin and your permanent address at the right-hand margin, two or three lines beneath your name. Even if you do not plan to move back home, you should list your permanent address. This gives employers a chance to leave a message for you if they are unable to reach you for any reason.

Don't forget to include both phone numbers. If you live on campus, you may wish to buy or borrow an answering machine, assuming you have a private phone. Do not leave frivolous recordings with jammin' riffs from your favorite band on the answering machine for potential employers to hear.

Example

School Address	Permanent Address
1015 Commonwealth Avenue	507 North 6th Street
Apartment 16	Houston, Texas 77024
Boston, Massachusetts 02145	Phone: 713/555-1234
Phone: 617/555-1483	

3. Work Experience

Work experience is the meat and potatoes of a resume. Recruiters want to see some kind of work history because it demonstrates that you have a good work ethic. (And it shows that you know how to get a job!) Remember, volunteer work, internships, and part-time experience are also important. (Please note that if you are still a student or your work experience is particularly weak, you can put your education section first, followed by your work experience. Whichever order you choose, the fundamentals will be the same.)

If, during college, you spent a summer traveling, studying, or performing some other enlightening or substantive activity rather than working, be sure to include this information. Recruiters hate to see gaps in resumes. They might assume that you sat on the beach for the entire summer or even fear that you have a medical or other personal problem that will interfere with your ability to work.

Always be truthful on your resume. In addition to the ethical arguments, more and more companies are checking resumes these days. Remember, false information on a resume is often considered grounds for dismissal. This can happen even if the falsehood is discovered years after you are hired. Nonetheless, your resume is essentially an advertisement for yourself, and you have every right to put your best foot forward and show your strongest points. Choosing which positions to list and highlight on your resume is an important part of creating a positive advertisement for yourself.

a. List your dates of employment with each company on the left. For summer positions, the word "summer" followed by the year is sufficient. For part-time work, you may list the year(s) or starting and ending month and year.

b. To the right of the dates of employment, list the company name, city, and state. Make sure all listings are aligned with the one above. In other words, if you use one tab between the date and the company name on your first listing, do so for all the rest.

Using tabs is much easier than using the spacebar. If the preset tabs in your word processor are in awkward positions and it's making your resume look funny, you can adjust the position of the tabs. If you're using Microsoft Word, you can add extra tabs simply by clicking on the ruler near the top of your document where you want a new tab to go. If you don't like that spot, simply click and hold on that tab, and drag it off the screen. You can also look in the Format pull-down menu under Tabs.

You have another choice for placement of the company name. You may choose to put the employer listing on the next line, as in the example below.

1999–present
DATA PUNCH ASSOCIATES, INC. Houston, Texas

c. On the next line, list your job title.

Example
Mail clerk and courier

d. On the next line describe the duties and responsibilities of your position. If you have several positions to list and are running out of room, go into the most detail on the positions that are most directly related to the position you are applying for. If all of your jobs are in the field of interest, list the most recent in the most detail. For now, list them all out in as much detail as you can. It's always easier to cut information when you have too much than try to add details later when there is space to fill.

Remember, your resume is an advertisement for yourself to open doors for interviews. You should focus on presenting those aspects of your position that speak most positively of your experience. Do not feel compelled to summarize the entire position or even to list your major duties as though you were writing a formal job description.

An even better idea than listing job duties is to focus on accomplishments or achievements, even if they are only small ones. For example, for a summer lifeguard position, a brief summary of your duties might read: "Supervised waterfront for busy public beach; responsible for safety of bathers, maintaining public order and cleanliness of the beach and parking areas." But is this enough?

While this description of your work might, at first glance, make the position of lifeguard sound more impressive than simply writing "Lifeguard at public beach," it does nothing to distinguish you from any other person who worked as a lifeguard. It would be much more effective to list an on-the-job accomplishment or achievement, even a minor one. For example, if you set up a box beside the trash can to collect paper or bottles and cans for recycling, you could replace the previous job description with, "Established recycling program for bottles and cans." This shows motivation, effort, and initiative beyond the basic duties of the position.

Example

A. → 1999–present
B. → DATA PUNCH ASSOCIATES, INC. Houston, Texas
C. → **Mail clerk and courier**
D. → Reorganized mail distribution and sorting system in the department.
Delivered sensitive documents to the executive department.
Established envelope recycling bins. ← **NOTE ACCOMPLISHMENT**

A. → 1998–99
PROMOTIONS ARE GOOD TO MENTION.
B. → SAM'S BEEFBURGERS Houston, Texas
C. → **Short-order cook**
D. → Began work as dishwasher. Promoted to short-order cook.
Opened restaurant, handled cash receipts, and supervised and trained new kitchen staff.

(Important note: Please remember the letters "A., B., C., etc." are here solely for you to follow along and should NOT appear on your final resume!)

Part-time Jobs

If you have part-time positions, you should include only the ones you held for at least six months. You want to avoid appearing like a job-hopper. Be selective in the part-time positions you list. Stress those that are the most relevant to your career: those that show initiative, those that are interesting, or those you held for the longest period of time.

Generally, you'll want to devote little space to part-time positions in comparison to full-time positions, unless the part-time positions are unusually significant experiences, such as work in the industry of your choice.

Part-time positions should be described in a format virtually identical to full-time positions. The only change you will make is adding the words *part-time* before or after the date. I usually recommend after so it's not the first thing a hiring manager sees.

Example

A.━━➤ 1997–98   part-time
B.━━➤ Boston University Bookstore Boston, Massachusetts
C.━━➤ **Floor and stockroom clerk**
D.━━➤ Arranged merchandise displays, handled customer service, and checked packing slips against shipments.

4. Education

a. Now you should list where you went to college, technical school, or other higher education (we'll talk about high school in a minute).

Example

1994–98
BOSTON UNIVERSITY Boston, Massachusetts

If you have not yet graduated and are currently working toward a degree (either full-time or part-time), you should begin with the phrase "Candidate for the degree of...."

If you have already graduated, you should begin "Awarded the degree of..."

If you did not graduate and are not currently pursuing your degree, you should simply list the dates you attended and the courses studied. For example, "Studied mathematics, physics, chemistry, and statistics."

Not yet graduated:
Candidate for the degree of _____ in
_____ (month/year), majoring in _____.

Already graduated:
Awarded _____ degree in _____
(month, year), majoring in _____.

Did not graduate, not currently pursuing degree:
Studied _____ (list key courses or subjects) and other
courses (or subjects) from _____ (dates).

Example

1994–98
BOSTON UNIVERSITY Boston, Massachusetts
Bachelor of Arts in mathematics.

If you are out of school and have been for at least a year, you can stop here
and move on to section 5, Personal Background. The only other element of your
education that you may want to list is c. your grade point average, but only if it's
really impressive. If you're still in school or have just graduated, continue reading
this section.

b. Courses
If you are out of school, you should not list courses you took in school. If you
are still in school, you may list your courses, but only mention the relevant ones.
If you're applying as a computer programmer, for example, chances are the hiring
manager isn't going to give a hoot about your Birdcalls 101 class.
Courses include _____, _____,
_____, _____, and
_____.

c. Grade point average
Next, you should list your grade point average (GPA). You should not
include a GPA below 3.0 on a 4.0 scale or below a B- on a letter scale.

Example

1994–98
BOSTON UNIVERSITY Boston, Massachusetts
Bachelor of Arts in mathematics.

Courses included statistics and computer programming. 3.4 grade point average.

If your GPA in your major was much higher than your overall GPA, you should include this information with or without your overall GPA.

Example
3.8 grade point average in major.
If you're still in school or decide to expand the education section, you have the option of listing your grade point average after any of the following items as well.

d. Class Rank
If you ranked extremely high in your class (generally within the top ten), you should include it in your resume.

Example
Ranked 3 in a class of 140 students.

e. Academic Achievements, Special Projects
Especially if you are unable to list a notable academic honor, it is a good idea to list a special project that you may have worked on. It may be a project that required only a few days of your time, but it could be important if it shows initiative in the academic area that has been the main focus of your college career.

Example
Conducted an independent research study on the effect of television on pre-adolescent children.
If you did not perform a special project, you may wish to list your senior thesis, if you wrote one, or your minor field of study. Make it clear to the reader of your resume that even though you didn't necessarily graduate at the top of your class, you were a quick study and an eager participant in the academic process. Your thesis can also appear before your grade point average.

Example
Thesis topic: "New Application of Co-Linear Coordinates."

f. Notable Academic Honors

Next, you should list any special academic awards, honors, or competitive scholarships. The following is an example that includes all of the elements from this section thus far. Remember, this is an example for someone who is still in school or only recently graduated. The full resume at the end of this chapter won't include all of these details in the education section because he has been out of school and has held a couple of jobs.

Education
1994–98
BOSTON UNIVERSITY Boston, Massachusetts
A. ➤ Candidate for the degree of Bachelor of Arts in June 1999, majoring in
B. ➤ mathematics. Courses include statistics and computer programming.
C. ➤ 3.4 grade point average. Ranked 3 in a class of 140.   ◄————— **D.**
E. ➤ Thesis topic: "New Applications of Co-Linear Coordinates."
F. ➤ Awarded the Elliot Smith Scholarship in 1997.

g. Extracurricular Activities

Even if you have glowing academic credentials, it is essential to list some extracurricular activities. (Remember, if you've been out of school for over a year, you should have skipped this part and should be reading section 5, Personal Background.) This demonstrates that you are sociable, get along well with people, and that you will easily adjust to the many different people you might encounter in the workplace. Extracurricular activities help a recruiter perceive you as a "low-risk" hire.

At the same time, by carefully choosing the extracurricular activities you list, you can help set yourself apart from the competition and move closer to the job you want. The key is selectively choosing and developing a limited range of activities. (You may want to choose only one activity.)

Avoid simply listing many sports or clubs haphazardly. This might give the impression that you start many projects with enthusiasm but don't finish them. Furthermore, in the small space available on your resume, you will only have room to describe a few items. If you include too many, you will give no indication of the depth of interest in any one activity. (Interests that you choose not to include under extracurricular activities can be included toward the bottom of your resume under the heading "Personal Background.")

Example

Treasurer of the Mathematics Club. Responsible for $7,000.00 annual budget. Co-chairperson of Boston University's semiannual symposium on "The Future of Mathematics." Exhibitor and prize winner at local photography shows. Helped to establish university darkroom.

h. High School

Including high school information on your resume is optional, unless of course you're still in high school. I'll talk about that in a moment. If you have made exceptional achievements in college and in your summer or part-time jobs, you should probably include these in your resume and omit your high school information. Most college graduates don't include their high school information on their resumes, but there are sometimes good reasons to do so.

If you do decide to include your high school achievements on your resume, describe them more briefly than your college achievements. Even if they are very impressive, putting too much emphasis on your high school years may give the impression that your highest performance days were in the past. Notice the following example uses the basic format you used for your higher education listing.

Example

> 1990–94
> HOUSTON PUBLIC HIGH SCHOOL Houston, Texas
> Received diploma in June 1994. Achieved Advance Placement
> standing in calculus and physics. Academic Honors all terms.
> Assistant Editor of school yearbook.

If you're still in high school or are a recent graduate, follow the format I outlined above for listing college experience as closely as you can. Also, you should list jobs held just like anyone else using the above format as well.

5. Personal Background

Listing personal interests should not be a priority. If you can fill your resume with good work experience and impressive educational accomplishments, then you should not worry so much about listing personal interests. There are some exceptions, however. If your personal interests are consistent with the job you are applying for and with the overall theme you are creating for your resume, then you can feel good about listing them.

If for example you're applying to be a book editor and you have read every Shakespeare play three times, then put down that you like reading Shakespeare. If you're applying to be a carpenter, and you love building birdhouses, then go ahead and put that down.

Remember to be consistent with whatever you put down. Also, do not include any personal information that people can use to discriminate against you.

Don't list your age, weight, height, race, marital status, sexual orientation, or anything else someone may use as an excuse to not give you the job. We would all like to think that a hiring manager would never discriminate, but it does happen.

Example
> PERSONAL BACKGROUND
> Enjoy photography, reading science fiction, and playing bridge.
> Published two articles in mathematics journals.

6. References

You should not list references on the resume for two reasons: it looks less professional, and it's good for you to know beforehand when a reference will be called. Not listing them on your resume also enables you to change or vary the references. Most people used to write "References available upon request," but I recommend that you don't do this. Hiring managers simply assume that you will have references.

That's it! Unless you've been writing things down as you went, you should now get your pen and paper ready and go through this section again. As you start each section, write down the important information the way you would like it to appear on your resume. You will then have the completed text for a complete resume that looks great!

The following is an example of a completed resume. You'll notice it includes most of the elements we went through step-by-step in this chapter. The person in this example has been out of school for over a year, so I left out some of the education details that would appear on a student's resume.

STEVEN M. PHILLIPS
507 North 6th Street
Houston, TX 77024
Phone: 713/555-1234

EXPERIENCE
1999–present
DATA PUNCH ASSOCIATES, INC. Houston, Texas
Mail Clerk and Courier
Reorganized mail distribution and sorting system in the department.
Delivered sensitive documents to the executive department. Established
envelope recycling bins.

1998–99
HARVEY'S BEEFBURGERS, INC. Houston, Texas
Short-order cook
Began work as a dishwasher. Promoted to short-order cook. Opened
restaurant, handled cash receipts, and supervised and trained new
kitchen staff.

1997–98 part-time
BOSTON UNIVERSITY BOOKSTORE Boston, Massachusetts
Floor and Stockroom Clerk
Arranged merchandise displays, handled customer service, and checked
packing slips against shipments.

1997–98 part-time
BOSTON UNIVERSITY Boston, Massachusetts
Tutor
One of six students invited to tutor for the Department of Mathematics.
Graded student papers and worked as a Research Assistant in Theoretical
Calculus.

EDUCATION
1994–98
BOSTON UNIVERSITY Boston, Massachusetts
Bachelor of Arts in mathematics. 3.4 grade point average.

PERSONAL BACKGROUND
Enjoy photography, reading science fiction, and playing bridge.
Published two articles in mathematics journals.

CHAPTER SEVEN

Over Thirty Real-World Examples of Job-Winning Resumes

This chapter is broken up into three sections. The first section features resumes for high-school students, college students, and recent graduates. The second section contains resumes for many common jobs that you may be applying for. The third section contains resumes for people in special situations who may have specific issues to deal with.

Even if you don't find the exact job you're looking for in this chapter, you'll notice that they all follow the basic format. Find the position that is the closest to the one you are applying for and use it as a model. Even if you find the exact job here, you may want to scan through some of the others to get a better feel for how resumes are put together.

I've added comments to each one that reflect what I feel is good about the resume, questions you should be prepared to answer, or just my general thoughts on job hunting. If you see that something is different about the resume, compare it to the basic format I gave you and think about why something might be different. Remember, as you create your resume, you're going to be choosing what you want to highlight. If something receives more attention on a resume, it's because the person decided that was what he or she wants the hiring manager to notice.

COLLEGE STUDENT APPLYING FOR AN INTERNSHIP

CHRIS SMITH

School Address:
178 Green Street
Skidell, LA 70458
(504) 555-5555

Permanent Address:
23 Blue Street
New Orleans, LA 70128
(504) 555-5555

OBJECTIVE
A summer internship in the book-publishing industry.

SUMMARY OF QUALIFICATIONS
- Copyediting: Two years' experience copyediting monthly church newsletter using *Chicago Manual of Style*
- Proofreading: Familiar with proofreading symbols
- Prolific writer; voracious reader

EDUCATION
TULANE UNIVERSITY, New Orleans, LA. **Bachelor of Arts in English and American Literature** with a concentration in film. Degree to be awarded May 1999. Dean's list. GPA in major: B+

EMPLOYMENT
THE NEW ORLEANS PEOPLE FIRST PROGRAM, Skidell, LA   1997-present
Adult Literacy Tutor
Travel to various prisons, nursing homes, boardinghouses, and learning centers. Tutor residents in elements of spelling, grammar, and parts of speech. Issue progress reports, bestow awards.

TULANE UNIVERSITY, New Orleans, LA   1996 -present
Manager, film series
Booked and publicized weekly films, arranged for projectionist and ticket taker, maintained accounts, paid bills.

TULANE MAILROOM, New Orleans, LA   Spring 1995
Mail sorter
Routed mail to appropriate departments and individual mailboxes (incoming); sorted mail by zip code (outgoing).

SKILLS
Computer: Word, Excel, QuarkXPress
Language: Intermediate-level French, American Sign Language

This is one case where an objective may be helpful. If this person isn't even close to graduating, then the objective makes it clear that he or she is only applying for an internship rather than a full-time position. Also, as an editor, I can tell you that computer skills are necessary at most companies, especially a book publisher. If you don't know the basics (at least one word processor and spreadsheet program), you should take a course at your school or state employment center.

Chris Smith
178 Green Street
Goshen, IN 46526
(219) 555-5555
csmith@netmail.com

EDUCATION
United States Naval Academy, Annapolis, MD
B.S. Computer Science, 1999
Curriculum emphasized analytical and technical skills for identifying, studying, and solving informational problems in business organizations.

COMPUTER SKILLS
- Programming in C++, Java, and BASIC
- Hardware-oriented courses: Microprocessors
- Software-oriented courses: Programming in BASIC, Operating Systems, File Structures, DATA Structures, Database Techniques, and Software Engineering
- Analysis and Design courses: Systems Analysis, Systems Design, and Programming Languages

EXPERIENCE
Summers 1998-99
The Let It Rise Restaurant, Goshen, IN
Waited tables, acted as host; developed good personal relation skills. Received deliveries and supplies and distributed them throughout the restaurant. Managed inventory.

Summer 1997
The Squeaky Cleaners, Goshen, IN
Shift supervisor responsible for staff of six. Handled and tallied cash receipts. Oversaw pickup and drop-off of clothing.

COLLEGIATE
United States Naval Academy is the nation's oldest private military college, which places demands upon its students beyond academic curriculum. The Academy develops leadership and organizational skills through a disciplined environment.

Charter Member of the Association for Computing Machinery (ACM)

Member of the USNA Division 1 Crew Team

Computer majors and others applying for computer positions must list their computer knowledge, skills, and experience in detail. Since this person doesn't have any work experience related to computers, he or she decided to list other positions held, which is a good idea, because a ten-line resume looks really, really silly.

ENGLISH MAJOR

Chris Smith
178 Green Street
Columbia, MO 65201
(314) 555-5555

OBJECTIVE
A position in the publishing field.

SUMMARY OF QUALIFICATIONS
- Four years' publishing experience.
- Proven writing skills; authored hundreds of pages of fiction and nonfiction in the past three years.
- Excellent communication abilities; lectured to a wide variety of audiences in a museum setting.

EDUCATION
DOWLING COLLEGE, Oakdale, NY
B.A., English, *magna cum laude*, 1999

SKILLS
Computer: Word, Excel, QuarkXpress, PageMaker
Languages: Bilingual in English and Spanish; some knowledge of French

COLLEGE ACTIVITIES
Plume, Literary Magazine   Fall 1995-Spring 1999
Editor (from Spring 1997), Production and Business Coordinator
Composed magazine budget and arranged specifications with printers.

Freelance Writer   Spring 1996-Spring 1999
Published book and movie reviews, essays, and stories in campus publications.

WORK EXPERIENCE
The Damien House Museum, Oakdale, NY   Spring 1999
Museum Assistant
Interpreted exhibits for visitors. Prepared and delivered short talks on historical subjects. Participated in organizing creative educational programs.

Bindings Bookstore, Oakdale, NY   Fall 1997
Sales Clerk/Floor Person
Maintained stock; helped customers make selections; registered sales.

Since this person's college activities are directly related to the industry in which he/she is looking for a job, it's okay to list them in more detail. Here's another example of an objective, just so you can see what it looks like in case you decide to use it. Notice, however, that it doesn't contain any of the phrases that make me want to gag like "team player," "detail-oriented person," or "a position that will challenge me."

HIGH SCHOOL GRAD (Child Care)

Chris Smith
178 Green Street
Jamaica, NY 11451
(718) 555-5555

WORK HISTORY

1998-present   Governess
MR. AND MRS. KURT URBANE
15 Goldstone Road, Jamaica, NY
- Provide full-time care for a 6-year-old girl.
- Duties include dressing, tutoring, chauffeuring, running errands, housework, cooking, and seeing to the child's needs and well-being.
- Live-in position.

1997   Governess
MR. AND MRS. PAUL McMAHON
145 Nicole Lane, Kutztown, PA
- Provided care for three children: an infant, a 3-year-old girl, and a 5-year-old boy.
- Live-in position.

1993-97   Babysitter
MR. AND MRS. STEVE McGYVER
333 Sunshine Court, Loveland, CO
- Provided care for an infant girl and toddler twin brothers.

SKILLS

- Valid driver's license; perfect driving record
- CPR/first aid certified
- Skiing, reading, horseback riding, traveling, swimming

EDUCATION

Boulder High, Boulder, CO

In this case, Chris's personal interests may be relevant to the position, and her skills definitely are important. When I babysat for a family of four, I thought I should know CPR and basic first aid. By the time it had occurred to me, I was ready to go back to college. If you're serious about child care, learning CPR is a good idea. Also, this person should be ready to answer the questions, "Are you planning on going to college?" and/or "Why don't you want to go to college?"

CHRIS SMITH
178 Green Street
Dahlonega, CA 31597
(404) 555-5555

SUMMARY OF QUALIFICATIONS
- Eight years' experience and broad-based knowledge of the accounting field.
- Proficient with Lotus 1-2-3; general ledger, accounts receivable and payable, auditing and cash flow functions.
- Strong numerical and administrative abilities.
- Experience training incoming personnel.

EXPERIENCE

1999-present   SAVANNA COMPTROLLER'S OFFICE, Dahlonega, CA
Accounting Assistant
- Monitor funding and financial reporting associated with various federal sponsors.
- Perform internal cost audits of terminated research contracts and grants.
- Coordinate audit and cash flow functions between CAO and other university departments.
- Create financial reports, monthly and quarterly reports, required governmental reports, and correspondence.

1996-99   NOSTRADAMUS CORPORATION, Dahlonega, CA
Accounting Assistant
- Held complete responsibility for receivables and payables.
- Computerized financial reports and auditing.
- Served as telephone and personal contact in customer service and in resolving problems with purchasing department.
- Maintained computer master files and related input data.

EDUCATION
CREIGHTON UNIVERSITY, Omaha, NE
Coursework in accounting, statistics, corporate finance, business law, and computers

COMPUTER SKILLS
Lotus 1-2-3, Excel, Word, WordPerfect, Access, dBase

By putting qualifications and jobs first, this resume says, "Hey, focus on my qualifications." This person listed relevant courses completed to show that even though she didn't finish school, she has a good background in the field. Even so, this person should be prepared to answer questions about why she did not or does not want to finish college.

CHRIS SMITH
178 Green Street
Dillon, MT 59725
(406) 555-5555

EDUCATION
BURDAN COLLEGE, Missoula, MT
- Candidate for B.A. in Criminal Justice, expected 2000.
- President of Christiansen Hall; manage budget of $800.

EXPERIENCE
YOUR STORE, Dillon, MT   1999-present
Cashier
- Provide customer and personnel assistance.
- Handle cash intake, inventory control, and light maintenance.
- Train and schedule new employees.
- Instituted store recycling program benefiting the Dillon Homeless Shelter.

RONDELL IMAGE, Helena, MT   1998-99
Data/File Clerk
- Assisted sales staff.
- Performed general office tasks, including data entry, typing, and filing invoices.

TARPY PERSONNEL SERVICES, Bozeman, MT   1997-98
General Clerk
- Handled shipping and receiving
- Filed invoices.

TELESTAR MARKETING, Great Falls, MT   1995-97
Telephone Interviewer
- Conducted telephone surveys dealing with general public and preselected client groups in selected demographic areas.
- Consistently placed within top 10 percent for number of surveys administered.
- Received Associate of the Month award twice and Outstanding Service Certificate.

True or False: Typewritten resumes (produced on a typewriter) are okay for entry-level retail positions. False! This may have been accepted at one point, but today there is no reason why a person can't find a computer to print a resume. If you skipped the beginning chapters of this book, then you also skipped some helpful suggestions on what to do if you don't have your own computer! (See page 28, Typing)

COACH

CHRIS SMITH
178 Green Street
Orono, ME 04473
(207) 555-5555

EXPERIENCE
University of Maine, Orono, Maine   1999-present
Assistant Varsity Hockey Coach
- Goaltender coach.
- Lead drills and practice.
- Coach individual team members in shooting, passing, and goaltending.
- Set up playing strategies.
- Scout opposing teams in preparation for games.
- Recruit potential student athletes.

Saint Joseph's College, North Windham, Maine   1998-99
Assistant Varsity Hockey Coach
Same responsibilities as in current position.

State Hockey School of Maine, Augusta, Maine   1994-97
Hockey Instructor, summer program

Maxfield All-American Hockey School, Orono, Maine   1993
Hockey Instructor

National Sports Camp of America at University of Maine, Orono, Maine   1992
Hockey Counselor and Instructor

EDUCATION
University of Maine, Orono, Maine
M.S. in Human Movement, Health, and Leisure, 1997
B.S. in Human Movement, Health, and Leisure, 1991

HONORS AND AWARDS
- Captain, NCAA Division I Champions, 1991
- Starting Varsity Hockey Goaltender, 1988-91
- All-East, 1988
- All-Star Goaltender, Bangor Tournament, 1988
- Outstanding Goaltender, Portland Tournament, 1988

Notice this resume doesn't contain anything that's not related to the specifics of coaching or playing on a team. It's clear what this person is all about and what he or she is looking for.

CHRIS SMITH
178 Green Street
Delaware City, DE 19706
(302) 555-5555

EXPERIENCE
Head Teacher: City Child Care Corporation, Delaware City, DE
September 1999-present
- Taught educational and recreational activities for 20 children, ages 5-10, in a preschool/daycare setting.
- Planned and executed age-appropriate activities to promote social, cognitive, and physical skills.
- Developed daily lesson plans.
- Observed and assessed each child's development. Conducted parent/teacher orientations and meetings.

Teacher: Little People Preschool and Daycare, New Castle, DE
June 1998-August 1999
- Taught educational and recreational activities for children, ages 3-7, in a preschool/daycare setting.
- Planned, prepared, and executed two-week units based on themes to develop social, cognitive, and physical skills.
- Taught lessons and activities in Mathematics, Language Arts, Science, and Social Studies.

Student Teacher: Rolling Elementary School, Newark, DE
January-May 1998
- Taught and assisted a kindergarten teacher in a self-contained classroom of 28 students. Planned and taught lessons and activities in Mathematics, Science, and Social Studies.

Teaching Intern
Freud Laboratory School, Newark, DE   January-May 1996
Green Meadow Elementary School, Newark, DE   January-May 1995
Delaware State College Daycare Centers, Dover, DE   October-December 1994

EDUCATION
University of Delaware, Newark, DE
B.A. in Early Childhood Education; GPA in Major: 3.5/4.0

CERTIFICATION
Delaware State, K-5

It's good to see someone with a clear career path. I realize your history may not be as seamless as this one. Notice the person has included all relevant information including student teaching positions, internships, and certifications.

FAST FOOD WORKER

Chris Smith
178 Green Street
Carson City, NV 89703
(702) 555-5555

EMPLOYMENT
1999-present   THE PIZZA PALACE, Carson City, NV
Server
• Participate in opening of new store outlets.
• Assist with public relations, food service, and register control.
• Resolve conflicts in high-pressure environment.

1998-99   NEVADA TELEPHONE, Las Vegas, NV
Data Input/Repetitive Debts Collection/Commercial
• Established commercial accounts; verified records and old accounts for new
  service.
• Provided customer service; fielded inquiries.

Summers 1995-98   BLACKTHORN DAY CAMP, Plaston, NH
Recreation Director
• Planned, programmed, and supervised camp activities for summer outdoor education and
  camping services for juvenile coeds.
• Supervised cabin group, counseled, and instructed in aquatics, sports, and special events. Wrote
  weekly reports to parents.

1993-94   SISYPHUS GROCERY, Manchester, NH
Produce Manager
• Maintained produce inventory.
• Assisted with public relations and in-house advertising for special sales and events.

EDUCATION
MANCHESTER HIGH SCHOOL, Manchester, NH
Diploma, College Preparatory

Here's a good example of where a short education history should go last. I think it's a good idea to at least mention the high school diploma rather than leaving it off altogether. If you don't have a high school diploma, you can consider not putting an education section on your resume. You should, however, be up front with any hiring managers that ask you about your education background. Try to come up with some answers ahead of time that will offer solid reasons (quit school to raise younger siblings, entered the military, etc.).

FITNESS INSTRUCTOR

CHRIS SMITH
178 Green Street
Richmond, VA 23220
(804) 555-5555

EXPERIENCE
1999-present   THE BABY BOOM, Richmond, VA
Owner/Operator
- Provide comprehensive yet responsible exercise classes for pregnant women.
- Supervise staff of 12. Hire and train employees, manage payroll, schedule work shifts, administer billing.
- Maintain steady contact with each client's physician, to ensure absolute safety for her and the baby.

1997-99   DEE DEE LEE'S FITNESS PHANTASMAGORIA, Richmond, VA
Aerobics/Calisthenics Instructor
- Taught intensive aerobics, calisthenics, and stretching to coeducational classes of up to 25 adults in all physical conditions.
- Geared program toward intermediate and advanced levels.
- Used music as a motivational tool.

1995-97   UP AND AT 'EM STUDIO, Norfolk, VA
Manager/Exercise Instructor
- Handled all sales (telephone and direct), marketing and strategy development.
- Developed client referral network.
- Motivated clients to perform intensive calisthenics, yoga, and stretching; taught techniques.
- Handled bookkeeping and all business activities.

EDUCATION

WILLAMETTE UNIVERSITY, Salem, OR
Bachelor of Arts in English, Minor in Physical Education
Studies in Physiology, Anatomy, and Nutrition
Captain of Women's Gymnastic Team

AFFILIATION

Associate member of Women in Fitness Association, Richmond Chapter

PERSONAL INFORMATION

In excellent health; perform daily aerobics, Nautilus, and Universal workouts; run 5-10 miles a day; enjoy hiking

In this case you see that the Personal Information section works because it reinforces her skills and experience.

GUARD

CHRIS SMITH
178 Green Street
Sundance, WY 82729
(307) 555-5555

EXPERIENCE

THE FIELDSTONE BANK   Sundance, WY
Bank Guard
1999-present
• Ensure safety and security of customers, bank employees, and bank assets.

WILLOW MEAD ART MUSEUM   Wolf, WY
Security Guard
1996-99
• Patrolled, performed surveillance, and controlled facilities and areas. Maintained reports, records, and documents as required.

CITY OF ROCK SPRINGS POLICE DEPARTMENT   Rock Springs, WY
Property Clerk
1993-96
• Supervised security, transfer, and storage of personal effects and properties as evidence in trial and court cases.

CITY OF GILLETTE SCHOOL DEPARTMENT   Gillette, WY
Transitional Aide
1989-93
• Ensured safety of students and security of school property at Madison Park High School.

THUNDERBEAT CONSTRUCTION   Crowheart, WY
Weigher of Goods/Track Foreman
1988-91
• Weighed materials and supervised track construction at University of Wyoming.

EDUCATION
UNITED STATES COAST GUARD, Miami, FL
Certificate, Interactive Query Language
Certificate, Advanced PMIS
Certificate, Coast Guard WP School
Winter Park High School, Winter Park, FL

When you're applying for a position as a guard, you want to show that you've had experience in two areas, security and leadership. The first, security, is obvious. The second, leadership, shows you have the potential to command greater responsibilities. Also, I think listing the Coast Guard information on this resume is good because it helps beef up a limited education section and it is consistent with the overall "security" theme.

HAIRSTYLIST

CHRIS SMITH
178 Green Street
Menoken, ND 58558
(701) 555-5555

SUMMARY OF QUALIFICATIONS
- Skilled in various hair cutting techniques, such as texturizing
- Experienced with permanents, body waves, and spiral perms
- Named "Most Promising Hairstylist" by the *Bismarck Gazette*
- Coordinated promotional events with local radio stations, including The First Annual Much Ado About Hair-Do's and Don'ts

EXPERIENCE
1998-present
The Hair Studio, Mandan, ND
Hairstylist
- Cut client's hair in requested styles.
- Use prepared dyes or create coloring or streaking as desired.
- Perform waxing.
- Answer phones and schedule appointments.
- Style hair for local fashion shows: French braids, twists, floral weaves.
- Doubled base clientele within first 2 months.

1995-98
Hair America, McKenzie, ND
Hairstylist
- Performed duties as above.
- Manicured nails.
- Independently sold hair-care products.

EDUCATION
National Hair Academy, Bismarck, ND
Hair Styling Certification

Some state certifications are stricter than others. You should be sure to list all the duties you are certified for (hair, nails, facials, coloring, etc.). If you are applying to a job in another state, you should check whether you'll need to take any additional tests or courses.

CHRIS SMITH
178 Green Street
Decorah, IA 52101
(319) 555-5555

EXPERIENCE
HOMECARE INCORPORATED, Decorah, IA
1999-present   *Case Administrator*
- Manage the daily clinical operation of CPMS (Clozaril Patient Management System), monitor laboratory results, and manage staff. Recruited to program at its inception to develop, test, and implement new home-care system.
- Coordinate patient services, including blood draws and drug delivery. Monitor and report lab results to physicians for review and documentation. Assisted in selecting and developing office and pharmacy.
- Establish and maintain service schedule for staff consisting of RNs, LPNs, phlebotomists, and pharmacists. Assist in recruiting, selecting, and evaluating RNs, LPNs, and phlebotomists. Administer training and orientation for clinical staff.
- Generate monthly Quality Assurance reports and audit records and computer files. Identify and resolve service-related incidents. Report and maintain record of incidents as described by quality assurance guidelines. Support marketing and sales teams of pharmaceutical companies.

1998   *Nurse Clinician*
- Provided professional nursing support for homebound patients in need of infusion therapy. Worked closely with Nursing Supervisor, agency staff, and referring physicians.
- Attended to full range of patients, including those with AIDS. Provided patient and family/caregiver education. Educated members of nutrition support, oncology, and IV teams in providing professional services.

SIOUX CITY HOSPITAL, Sioux City, IA
1994-98   *Staff nurse* for the medical/surgical units
- Assessed condition of primary-care patients. Planned and implemented services, evaluated patient outcomes.
- Acted as resource nurse for staff of a 50-bed unit, with immediate responsibility for 12–15 patients.
- Supervised LPNs and ancillary staff.

LICENSE
Registered Nurse, State of Iowa, #379526

EDUCATION
SIOUX CITY HOSPITAL SCHOOL OF NURSING, Sioux City, IA
B.S. in Nursing

Here's a good example of when to put the education section last. This person's practical work experience is very strong, so it should come first. Also, don't forget to put other pieces of important information like any licenses or affiliations.

NANNY

Chris Smith
178 Green Street
Livermore, CO 80536
(303) 555-5555

EXPERIENCE

1999-present   Private residence, Livermore, CO
NANNY
Care for twin boys from the age of two months through two years. Assist in selecting toys and equipment, provide environmental stimulation, personal care, and play.

1997-99   Baby Bear Preschool, Keystone, CO
TEACHER
Taught infant, preschool, and after-school programs. Planned curriculum, organized activities, communicated with parents and staff regarding children's growth and development. Suggested equipment to enrich children's experiences and helped create a stimulating environment.

1995-97   This Little Piggy Daycare Center, Dove Creek, CO
TEACHER
Planned and implemented curriculum for infants. Communicated with parents and other staff regarding daily progress of children.

1993-95   The Kid Corral, Wild Horse, CO
TEACHER
Planned and implemented curriculum for toddler program. Enriched children's experiences through play, music, and art.

1991-93   Ivywild Coalition for Retarded Citizens, Ivywild, CO
CAREGIVER
Provided care in clients' homes, administering physical therapy when necessary. Planned activities to stimulate and improve children's skills and environment.

EDUCATION

Metropolitan State College, Denver, CO
Completed 30 credits in Education, with an emphasis on the daycare setting.
Minor: English.

SKILLS

Valid driver's license; perfect driving record
CPR/first aid certified
Skiing, reading, music, arts and crafts

Why didn't this person put his/her available references on here? Won't most people ask a nanny for references? Yes. That's why putting it on your resume is redundant and unnecessary. Remember, that goes for *all* resumes. One thing I really like about this resume is that the person is CPR certified. If you are, definitely put it on your resume if you're applying for a job where it could come into play (nanny, lifeguard, flight attendant, etc.).

NURSE (Home Health Care)

Chris Smith
178 Green Street
Yukon, MO 65589
(314) 555-5555

EXPERIENCE

1999-present   **AIDS Clinical Coordinator/Home Infusion Nurse**
THE LAMONT CENTER   Yukon, MO
- Provide case management, teaching, and follow-up for AIDS patients receiving home infusion therapies.
- Identify appropriate candidates for high-tech home infusion therapies.
- Train patients and families to safely conduct these complex therapies at home.
- Therapies include total parenteral and enteral nutrition, IV antibiotic therapy, infusion chemotherapy, parenteral pain management, and IV hydration.

Achievements
- Identified need for study on the infection rate of venous access devices in AIDS patients; currently collecting pertinent data.
- Appointed to the Lamont Center Home Care Committee.

1993-99   **Senior Staff Nurse (Level II)**
Oncology Division
- Functioned as primary nurse coordinating care for acute and chronic patients.
- Provided nursing care for chemotherapy and pain-management patients.
- Facilitated discharge planning with home-care agencies.
- Acted as coordinator for autologous bone-marrow transplant program.
- Conducted inservices for staff on procedural updates and progress of program.
- Served as hospital oncology resource for care of central venous catheters.

Achievements
- Developed orientation program for new staff members.
- Served as chair of the Family Education Committee.

LICENSE
Registered Nurse, State of Missouri #794791

EDUCATION
Building Professional Skills to Work with Intravenous Drug Users
AIDS Program for Clinical Nurses

RENDALL HOSPITAL SCHOOL OF NURSING, Saint Louis, MO
Diploma: Registered Nurse

Sometimes all your information won't fit on one page. Unless you're a high-level executive, you shouldn't go over one page. In this example, Chris concentrated on her most recent jobs and left off older and irrelevant positions.

ORDER ENTRY CLERK

CHRIS SMITH
178 Green Street
Lincoln, NE 68522
(402) 555-5555

EXPERIENCE
THE BULLFROG COMPANY, Lincoln, NE   1999-present
Order Entry Clerk, Parts Department
- Process and ship orders within 12 hours of receipt to Bull Group Field Engineers in the U.S. and abroad.
- Consistently meet or exceed daily deadlines.
- Coordinate with multiple departments and shippers to ensure timely delivery.
- Establish and maintain functional files.
- Use computer to track orders and determine parts status and availability.
- Generate daily reports on status of orders.
- Use reports to identify and resolve order processing problems.
- Investigate and resolve complaints from Field Engineers.

K.T., INC., Norfolk, NE   1997-99
General Office Administrator
- Typed letters and reports, maintained files, answered inquiries about customer accounts.
- Received payments and balanced statements. Posted accounts receivable and payable.
- Supervisor said I had displayed one of the finest first years she had ever seen.

EDUCATION
Marcelle Junior College, Omaha, NE
B.A., Computer Science, expected 2001.

COMPUTER SKILLS
Writing: Word, WordPerfect
Financial: Lotus 1-2-3, Excel
Other: Various proprietary database and order entry systems

Not only is this resume a good example for order entry clerks, but it's a pretty good example for someone who's still in school. Or maybe this person is working full-time and getting a degree at night. That's probably what's going on here because this person didn't list any awards or clubs. I mean who's got time for the chess club when you're working 40 hours a week and getting a degree at the same time?

PROOFREADER

CHRIS SMITH
178 Green Street
Hope, AR 71801
(501) 555-5555
csmith@netmail.com

EXPERIENCE

1999-present   Vigilant Widow Publishers, Hope, AR
Proofreader
- Proofread for small press.
- Mark for typographical errors and page makeup using standard proofreading symbols.
- Query suspected errors.
- Proofread bluelines prior to publication.
- Capable of rush jobs or longer-term assignments.

1995-99   Sapphire Business Forms, Walnut Ridge, AR
Proofreader
- Proofread outgoing business forms, pamphlets, booklets, and direct-mail pieces.
- Rewrite and copyedit if necessary.
- Proofread company Web site.

1993-95   Walsingham Press, Birmingham, AL
Secretary
- Answered phones, typed letters and memos, and provided customer service.
- In addition to secretarial functions, proofread outgoing business forms, pamphlets, and booklets.

EDUCATION
Krakotoa State Community College, Eureka, IL
B.A. in English

SKILLS
Computer
Word, WordPerfect, PageMaker

Other
Knowledge of *Chicago Manual of Style*

I know a lot of people out there want to be proofreaders, thinking it will be fun and easy. Saying that you read a lot of books is *not* a qualification publishers look for. It *is* fun, but it's not necessarily easy. Publishers look for good experience (who doesn't), an English major or minor, and any other training or courses taken. Think about your current and/or past jobs. Did you write any copy? Did you proofread the boss's memos? Even if you weren't technically a proofreader, focusing on these duties will help (see secretary position on this resume). If you can, take a proofreading course at the local community college, and brush up on your proofreader's symbols.

RECEPTIONIST (General)

CHRIS SMITH
178 Green Street
Laramie, WY 82071
(307) 555-5555

EMPLOYMENT
MARSTON CONVENT, Laramie, WY, 1998-present
Receptionist
Answer phone, greet visitors, and provide information, tours, and literature. Record and monitor thank-you notes for all received donations. Perform light typing, filing, and word processing.

RINALDO RANCH, Laramie, WY, 1993-98
Secretary
Provided word processing, customer relations, some accounts payable processing. Implemented new system for check processing; increased prompt payment of client bills.

WOMANPOWER INC., Laramie, WY, 1990-93
Secretary
Acted as liaison between public and CEO.

STATE HEALTH COALITION, Laramie, WY, 1986-90
Statistical Typist
Prepared health record documentation of infectious disease patients at State hospital. Trained new hires.

SKILLS
Computer
Word, WordPerfect, Excel, Lotus 1-2-3

Other
Typing (65 wpm), statistical typing, shorthand, dictaphone, multi-line phones/switchboard, book-keeping, credit checks

EDUCATION
TRAINING, INC., Boston, MA
Office careers training program in bookkeeping, typing, reception, word processing, and office procedures

ST. JOSEPH'S ACADEMY, Portland, Maine
Diploma

This resume is really strong because this candidate has highlighted relevant skills throughout the resume. All nonrelevant information has been left off.

CHRIS SMITH
178 Green Street
Kerryville, TX 78028
(512) 555-5555

EXPERIENCE
1997–99
RIP VAN WINKLE DAY CARE, Amherst, MA
Teacher Aide
Planned curricula for after-school programs, kindergarten through third grade. Organized field trips and also managed a day camp.

Summer 1997–98
GRAVEL ROAD RECREATION CENTER, Kerryville, TX
Assistant Recreation Leader
Responsible for planning and leading group recreational activities for 20 to 35 children, ages 7 to 14 at neighborhood youth center.

Summer 1996
STRAWBERRY HILL DAY CAMP, Prairie View, TX
Group Leader
Supervised teenage boys in recreational activities, including archery, riflery, swimming, and others. Supervised 10 to 25 children in the camp swimming pool. Won Group Leader of the Year award.

Summer 1995
PEBBLE BEACH DAY CAMP, Prairie View, TX
Physical Education Instructor
Taught dance and self-defense classes for teenagers in groups of 5 through 12.

EDUCATION
UNIVERSITY OF MASSACHUSETTS
Bachelor of Arts, History 1999
GPA 3.24, Academic Scholarship, Honor Society

UNIVERSITY OF TEXAS
Master's degree in Education, expected Spring 2001

I can tell a lot from this resume. I can see that either this person is currently not working while getting his/her master's or has chosen not to list an unrelated job. I see that Chris worked during college and also summers at home, and the good thing about all these jobs were that they are all related. Chris has good experience supervising children and teenagers.

TECHNICAL WRITER

CHRIS SMITH
178 Green Street
Melrose, FL 32666
(904) 555-5555
csmith@netmail.com

EXPERIENCE
1999-present   RIZZO ASSOCIATES, Melrose, FL
Technical Writer/Project Administration
- Research data and accurately describe the installation, removal, erection, and maintenance of all military hardware.
- Outline wiring diagrams and draw part breakdowns for illustrators.
- Serve as administration lead for specific projects in A-3, EA-3, and EP-3E programs.
- Work on IPB, MIM, and IFMM for all maintenance levels.
- Read from various source materials, including engineering drawings and wiring diagrams.

1994-99   CAPABIANCO PUBLISHING, Winter Park, FL
Technical Writer
- Performed duties as above for military hardware. Served as project lead, including editing, layout, and corrections. Started in Report Storage/Administrative Assistance; promoted to technical writer.

1992-94   DARK WILLOW ENGINEERING CORPORATION, Killarney, FL
Editor/Writer
- Edited and wrote large proposals for government contracts. Designed format and coordinated production. Organized and maintained up-to-date dummy book through several revision cycles. Interpreted client RFP requirements and determined applicability of proposal response to RFP.

EDUCATION
Curtis College, Winter Park, FL
B.S. in Civil Engineering
Coursework in English Composition, Drafting, and Computer Science.

COMPUTER SKILLS
Writing: Word, WordPerfect
Financial: Lotus 1-2-3, Excel
Other: CAD

Technical writing is a growing field. If you don't have the experience, you can still get an entry-level position if you have a writing or computer background.

TRAVEL AGENT

CHRIS SMITH
178 Green Street
Joliet, IL 60435
(815) 555-5555

SUMMARY OF QUALIFICATIONS
- Four years' experience acquired during employment and educational training within the travel industry.
- Thorough knowledge of various reservation transactions, including booking, bursting, ticketing, sales, customer service, and dealing with contracted vendors to ensure customer reservation specifications.
- Familiar with SABRE reservations system.
- Proficient at general office duties.

PROFESSIONAL EXPERIENCE
SURGE AND SIEGE TRAVEL, INC., Joliet, IL   1999-present
Air Coordinator
Coordinate air ticketing requests and tour departures using APOLLO and SABRE systems. Resolve client problems and special requests. Verify international and domestic fares; input pricing data. Issue tickets and final itineraries. Maintain and file pertinent materials. Assist with special projects; prepare reports.

GOTTA FLY TOURS, Wheaton, IL   1997-99
Computer Operator/Supervisor
Executed all SABRE operations. Administered ARC ticket stock and accountable documents. Managed office accounting. Supervised personnel. Served as group leader for Caribbean familiarization trips. Implemented system to eliminate SABRE computer costs.

QUICK TRIP TRAVEL, Evanston, IL   1996-97
Travel Consultant
Arranged individual and group travel. Generated invoices.

EDUCATION
MIDWEST TRAVEL SCHOOL, Chicago, IL
Graduated third in class, 1996.

DEPAUL UNIVERSITY, Chicago, IL
Bachelor of Arts, History, 1995.

WINDY CITY COMMUNITY COLLEGE, Chicago, IL
Associate of Arts, Geography, 1993.

This person chose to use a chrono-functional resume. The summary of qualifications represents the functional part. Chris shows that he or she is capable of carrying out the duties expected of a travel agent. The job listings represent the chronological part and display skills and duties consistent with the summary.

TUTOR

CHRIS SMITH
178 Green Street
Bel Air, MD 21015
(301) 555-5555

EDUCATION
Loyola College, Baltimore, MD
Bachelor of Arts in English: Professional Writing, *cum laude,* 1998
GPA: 3.21/4.0. Dean's List, 6 semesters

EXPERIENCE
Goden Academy, Baltimore, MD   January 1999-present
Tutor
Teach English to a Japanese senior 6 hours a week, concentrating on grammar and composition.

Ridge Heights Elementary, Baltimore, MD   November 1998-present
Teaching Assistant
Instruct group of 5 second- and third-grade students in writing and creative expression.

WPIT, Boston, MA   September 1998
News Intern
Spent a week in the newsroom, field reporting, and attending music and promotional meetings at Boston's #1 radio station. Communicated with traffic center and sourced news stories.

Loyola College, Baltimore, MD   Summer 1998
Writing Skills Tutor
Assisted students with writing and managed writing skills center during daily hours.

Camp Lalcota, Bethesda, MD   Summer 1997
Special Needs Counselor
Planned and supervised daily events. Assisted in care and feeding of campers ages 6-15.

Loyola College, Baltimore, MD   September 1997-May 1998
Peer Counselor
Assisted students in social and personal development regarding adjustment to college life. Led group and individual counseling sessions.

COMPUTERS
Word, Lotus 1-2-3

Since this person hasn't been out of school long, and since her educational accomplishments were quite impressive, Chris decided to list the Education section first. It works in this case because Chris knows that people want a tutor to be smart.

WAITPERSON

CHRIS SMITH
178 Green Street
Kaneohe, HI 96744
(808) 555-5555

EXPERIENCE

THE PALMS, Kaneohe, HI   1998-present
Head Waiter
• Managed, opened, and closed high-volume restaurant.
• Hired, trained, scheduled, and supervised wait staff.
• Reconciled cash intake.

PALUA SAILS RESTAURANT, Kaneohe, HI   1996-98
Head Waiter
• Provided efficient service to full bar and serving area.
• Trained new waitstaff.
• Chosen Employee of the Month.

CANDLE IN THE WIND, Honolulu, HI   1995-96
Barback
• Handled customer service and cash intake.
• Assisted with liquor inventory.
• Performed security services.

BLUE HAWAII RESTAURANT, Honolulu, HI   1994-95
Busboy
• Organized large dining room.
• Trained new bus people.

ADDITIONAL TRAINING
• Certified in the SIPS program for responsibly serving alcohol.
• Attended Restaurant Association training session: "Customer Satisfaction
  in the 90s."

EDUCATION
HAWAII LOA COLLEGE, Kaneohe, HI
B.A. in Liberal Arts, candidate, expected 2000

The additional training section on this resume works well because it reinforces the basic skills of a traditional waitperson. I would include a section like this on any resume where you can put together two or three additional certifications, courses, or programs that add value to your basic skill set.

CHRIS SMITH
178 Green Street
Austin, TX 78701
(512) 555-5555

EXPERIENCE
Web Site Manager, BusinessVillage.com LLC, Fort Bliss, Texas
November 1998–present
Direct the development, design, programming, and day-to-day operation of small business assistance Web site. Coordinate strategic relationships, marketing, and advertising campaigns to maximize traffic and revenue.

- Oversee daily operations and management of BusinessVillage.com.
- Research and select editorial materials for site content.
- Optimize page design for search engine ranking.
- Appraise effectiveness of site features to increase repeat users.
- Develop strategic alliances with complementing sites.
- Manage the production of non-Web promotional materials.
- Supervise and assist HTML, ASP, and PERL coding.

Manager, Shagwell Creek LLC, Freedom, Texas
November 1996–August 1998
Information Systems
- Developed a PC-based LAN for Financial and Purchasing departments.
- Instituted Kronos automated time clock for labor tracking.
- Provided technical support for PC, MAC, and AS400 users.

Marketing
- Designed Web pages to target new customers.
- Identified and located potential new retail outlets.
- Conducted market research on new product concepts.

EDUCATION
Master of Business Administration   May 1997
Powers University, Sharp, Texas

Bachelor of Arts, Psychology   May 1992
Swinger College, Flower Hill, Texas

This is a great-looking resume. The job listings use lots of action verbs and are very detailed. Each one also highlights the computer-related skills this person possesses.

WEBMASTER

CHRIS SMITH
178 Green Street
Newtown, PA 18940
(215) 555-5555

QUALIFICATIONS:
- Web Design & Development
- Intranet Design & Development
- HTML
- Multimedia Production
- Visual Basic Script
- Project Management
- Graphics Production
- Java Script
- Internet Information Server (IIS)

EXPERIENCE:
Webmaster (April 1997–Present)
Logical Works Inc., Princeton, NJ
Marketing Department
- Maintained and updated Logical Works Internet and Intranet sites.
- Designed and developed new customer oriented sections of Internet site including programming in Visual Basic script, Java script, and HTML.
- Interacted with various departments to design and develop departmental Intranet sites to provide information access to company employees.
- Generated Web site reports to track customer usage and usability of Web site to increase productivity of the Internet as a communications tool.

Associate Producer (September 1996–April 1997)
Cognet Corporation, Princeton Junction, NJ
Intern
- Designed and scripted a kiosk application for the United States Post Office.
- Developed programming specifications and programmed prototypes using Visual Basic 4.0.
- Coordinated production of graphics and interfaced with third-party software developers.
- Served as project manager for C.B.G. Spender Inc. Intranet Web site.

Web Designer & HTML Programmer (January 1996–August 1996)
University Relations, Bloomsburg University of Pennsylvania
Graduate Assistant
- Designed and programmed Bloomsburg University's Athletic Department Web pages.

EDUCATION:
Master of Science in Instructional Technology (December 1996)
Bloomsburg University of Pennsylvania, Bloomsburg, PA
Graduated *cum laude* 3.73/4.00

Bachelor of Arts in Mass Communications (August 1994)
Bloomsburg University of Pennsylvania, Bloomsburg, PA
Graduated *cum laude* 3.52/4.00

Webmasters are in high demand in today's world. If you're in computers or are still in school and have the time and the gumption to learn more about Web technology, I highly suggest you do. Even though I'm a book editor and author, I made it a point to teach myself HTML because it adds value to my resume.

CHRIS SMITH
178 Green Street
Huntington, WV 25702
(304) 555-5555

SUMMARY OF QUALIFICATIONS
Accomplished career counselor in the educational field
Extensive experience in management, including hiring and training
Good background in customer relations and human resources

EXPERIENCE
The Westview Schools, Huntington, WV
Career Counselor
1985-present
- Contact and interview potential candidates for business courses.
- Describe school programs and provide literature.
- Administer aptitude tests; advise prospective students as to their best courses to pursue.
- Organize welcoming ceremony and orientation meetings for new students each semester.
- Track completion and job-placement statistics.

Greenbriar Corporation, Huntington, WV
General Manager
1976-85
Greenbriar Corporation is a manufacturer of stamped metal parts.
- Selected, set up, equipped, and staffed new facilities. Supervised plant maintenance.
- Hired, trained, and supervised 18 skilled production personnel, 4 executives, and 16 support staff.
- Established incentive plans and quality, production, and cost controls.
- Supervised payroll, billing, credit and collection, purchasing, and finance for this $24 million company.

EDUCATION
Northeastern University, Boston, MA
Bachelor of Science in Business Administration
Concentration: Industrial Relations and Accounting

Age discrimination really surprises me. Older people often have great experience and are more likely to stay at your company for a longer time. Some companies don't want to hire older people because they usually command higher salaries. But what really costs more, hiring an older person at $15,000 more a year, or hiring new twenty-somethings every six months because they keep leaving? Training costs money too.

Chris Smith
178 Green Street
St. Louis, MO 63130
(314) 555-5555

EXPERIENCE
MARCA INFRARED DEVICES, St. Louis, MO
Manufacturers of infrared sensing and detecting devices.

Administrator   1998-present
Personnel
- Maintain engineering personnel status and monitor performance to plan.
- Automated weekly labor reports to calculate staffing levels and labor effectiveness.
- Train staff in library functions involving documentation ordering and CD-ROM usage.

Capital Expenditures
- Automated capital equipment planning cycle. Act as capital expenditure liaison for all of engineering.
- Perform year-end closeout on engineering purchase orders.

Budget Support
- Automated calculation of vacation dollars for engineering budget planning.
- Track contractor and consultant requisitions.

Documentation Control Clerk   1997-98
- Tracked and maintained changes to engineering documentation.
- Trained personnel in status accounting function and audit performance.

Documentation Specialist   1994-97
- Tracked and maintained changes to manufacturing and engineering documentation.
- Generated parts lists and was initial user of computerized bills of materials.
- Directed changes in material requirements to material and production control departments.

Configuration Management Analyst   1992-94
- Tracked and maintained changes to engineering documentation.
- Chaired Configuration Review Board.
- Presented configuration status reports at customer reviews.

Inside Sales Coordinator   1991-92
- Served as first customer contact.
- Directed customer calls and customer service.
- Maintained literature files and processed incoming orders.

EDUCATION
B.S. in Biology, Washington University

Personally, I don't see what the big deal is having all your experience at one company as long as you show that you were constantly learning, growing, and, most important of all, contributing to the bottom line. That's really the key.

CHRIS SMITH
178 Green Street
Holland, MI 49423
(616) 555-5555

SUMMARY OF QUALIFICATIONS
- Excellent interpersonal and communication skills; cooperative, patient, supportive, and loyal team player.
- Highly adaptable and comfortable with unconventional/alternative settings and situations; familiar with academic, domestic, and creative routines and structures.
- Ability to ensure a project or task is completed accurately and in a timely fashion; strong on follow-up.
- Energetic and vital; remain active member of community organizations while raising a large family.

EXPERIENCE
MICHIGAN MENTAL HEALTH CENTER, Detroit, MI   1998–present
Co-Leader, Substance Abuse Program
Assist the Day Hospital staff with transition patients; assist on a team therapy program with group modules in health awareness, gardening, and literature.

HOLLAND PUBLIC WORKS DEPT.   Summers 1986–present
Activities Coordinator
Supervise local children in crafts, sports, and games at the town playground. Requires knowledge of CPR and First Aid.

SHARONA REALTORS, Ypsilanti, MI   1985–86
Sales Representative

MICHIGAN STATE, East Lansing, MI   1983–85
Instructor, Art History
Developed curriculum; taught rudimentary aesthetics, method, and appreciation of modern American Art.

EDUCATION
DETROIT SCHOOL OF PHOTOGRAPHY, Detroit, MI.
Graduate, Applied Photography.

UNIVERSITY OF PENNSYLVANIA, Philadelphia, PA.
Bachelor and Master of Arts: History.

There are three keys to this resume. One is to focus on past job experience. The second is to list volunteer experience if it lends itself to the position being applied for. You don't have to put that it's volunteer work on the resume, but you should mention it if asked. The other is describing your day-to-day activities by their functional qualities. Look how taking little Jimmy to the playground for arts and crafts day suddenly becomes a supervisory role! And it's all true!

AT-HOME MOM REENTERING THE WORK FORCE
(Nursing)

CHRIS SMITH
178 Green Street
Upper Montclair, NJ 07043
(201) 555-5555

EXPERIENCE
MONTCLAIR MEMORIAL HOSPITAL, Montclair, NJ   1994-97
R.N. Staff Nurse
Addictions Treatment Program
Provide patient care on 40-bed mental health unit, administering medication, Emergency Room consulting, collaborating with health-care providers.
- Assess and evaluate patients in substance abuse crises. Conduct post-crisis interview and provide counseling.
- Assess medical complications.
- Collaborate with treatment team to implement inpatient and aftercare plans.
- Verify and pre-certify insurance providers.
- Lead and co-lead educational groups for patients and their families.

Staff Nurse/Psychiatric Addiction Emergency Service   1991-94
- Assessed addicted and psychiatric patients to determine severity of illness and level of care needed.
- Collaborated with health-care providers and medical team.

MONMOUTH COLLEGE/NURSING PROGRAM, West Long Branch, NJ   1989-91
Instructor/Medical Assisting Techniques
- Instructed students in the arts and skills of office medical procedures.
- Organized and planned curriculum, tested and graded students in written and practical methods.

CITY OF NEWARK SCHOOL DEPARTMENT, Newark, NJ   1987-89
Substitute School Nurse
- Administered first aid for students in K-12.
- Performed eye and ear testing. Provided counseling and health instruction.

LICENSE
Registered Nurse: Registration Number 10468

EDUCATION
JERSEY CITY HOSPITAL SCHOOL OF NURSING, Jersey City, NJ

The advice that goes for the at-home dad reentering the work force applies to the at-home mom. In this case, however, this woman's prior experience in the field is so strong, it isn't as necessary to translate everyday duties into functional experience.

CAREER CHANGER (Public Relations)

CHRIS SMITH
178 Green Street
Juneau, AK 99801
(907) 555-5555
csmith@netmail.com

SUMMARY
- Over 3 years' experience in public relations
- Proven ability to plan and supervise major special events
- Knowledge of all aspects of media relations
- Skilled educator and public speaker

EXPERIENCE
1998-present   ALASKANS FOR A CLEANER WORLD
Juneau, AK
Public Relations Coordinator (part-time)
- Handle all aspects of media relations.
- Plan and supervise special events. Organized first annual "Breath of Life" walk-a-thon, raising over $15,000.
- Educate public about environmental issues, including speaking at local schools.

1997-present   MT. JUNEAU MEDICAL CENTER
Juneau, AK
Coordinator, Department of Neurosurgery
- Promote department; oversee public relations.
- Coordinate communications for medical and nonmedical activities within department.
- Serve as liaison between administrations of two hospitals, physicians, and nurses.
- Educate in-house staff, patients, and families on techniques, equipment, and related subjects.

PRESENTATIONS AND LECTURES
Have given over 25 presentations and lectures to various schools, hospitals, in-house staff, and professional associations.

COMPUTER SKILLS
Windows, WordPerfect, Lotus 1-2-3, Excel

EDUCATION
UNIVERSITY OF ALASKA, Anchorage, AK
Bachelor of Science in Nursing

One of the keys to this resume is to show how the skills you've developed in other jobs can translate into the position you're applying for. You want to display a certain consistency. This candidate may have worked in different industries, but notice the consistency of skills and duties: public relations, promotions, event planning, etc.

DISPLACED HOMEMAKER (Food Service)

CHRIS SMITH
178 Green Street
Cheyenne, WY 82009
(307) 555-5555

SUMMARY
Award-winning country-style cook
Knowledge of commercial food preparation and service
Experience in quantity cooking

EXPERIENCE
Lion's Club Carnival, Cheyenne, WY
1994-present
Cook
Staff concession booths at annual carnival; prepare and serve such items as fried dough, sweet sausage, pizza, and caramel apples. Maintain a receipt record of profits for event administrators.

St. Bernadette's Parish, Cheyenne, WY
1996-present
Bake Sale Coordinator
Coordinate annual bake sale; provide approximately 10% of bakery items sold.

Payne Community Center, Cheyenne, WY
1999-present
Instructor
Conduct informal weekly cooking classes.

Jameson Homeless Shelter, Cheyenne, WY
1999-present
Weekday Server
Serve 200 lunches per day. Act as liaison between homeless guests and national food distributor, securing special requests and unanimously favored items.

AWARDS
First prize in national fruit-based pie competition
$100 *Reader's Digest* prize for best pot roast recipe

EDUCATION
Cheyenne Community College, Cheyenne, WY
Associate in Home Economics

This resume works because the candidate has emphasized his/her skills that can translate into the duties of the position he/she is applying for. Note the consistency. Everything centers around food and food-preparation skills. Even the Awards section highlights food-related accomplishments.

CHRIS SMITH
178 Green Street
Fort Worth, TX 76114
(817) 555-5555

EMPLOYMENT
WDDE Radio, Fort Worth, TX   1998–present
Copywriter/Service Director
Compose copy for advertisements and promotions. Edit client copy, client newsletter, and executive correspondence. Communicate with clients and listeners by phone. Produce commercials. Organize and oversee copy and taped spots. Assign on-air personalities for recording. Coordinate technical aspects of on-air programming.

Fairfield Mint, Fairfield TX   1997–98
Copywriter
Researched and wrote copy for Coins of the World, a 25-panel collector set. Conducted library research for projects on Jackie Robinson, the NFL's greatest games, and several other projects. Met all deadlines.

Texas Mutual Inc., Dallas, TX   1996–97
Claims Coder
Processed claims reports and encode data to computer system. Reviewed and revised reinsurance files. Conducted inventory. Balanced daily accounts for each computer system.

University of Dallas, Irvine, TX   1995–96
Mathematics Tutor
Tutored college students.

EDUCATION
Dave Erickson "Public Speaking" course
University of Dallas, Irvine, TX, B.S. in Education, *summa cum laude*; minor in English
Member of Kappa Kappa Gamma Honor Society

SPECIAL INTERESTS
Volunteer at Mi Casa, a Battered Women's Shelter (Dallas)

Even if you've changed jobs every year, you want to try to show some consistency (a common theme throughout this book). In this case, the candidate has tried to highlight his/her communication and copywriting skills, because that's the job he/she's applying for. Always remember to tailor your resume to the job you're applying for. Don't highlight your professional wrestling experience if you're applying as an accountant.

CHRIS SMITH
178 Green Street
Sumter, SC 29150
(803) 555-5555

Summary of Qualifications
More than 7 years' writing and editing experience
Adept at managing multiple responsibilities simultaneously
Experienced at delegating authority and motivating others to ensure efficiency and productivity

Work Experience
Editor-in-Chief, *Renegade* magazine, Sumter, SC   1996-99
Selected submissions, edited and wrote headlines for submissions and columns, laid out pages, recruited columnists, trained associates. Frequently performed copyediting and research.

Associate Editor, *Modern Daze*, New York, NY   1990-94
Wrote articles for both the magazine and its associated newsletter, Disembodied Voices. Edited features and department articles. Read and critiqued assigned articles from contributing editors.

Copyeditor, *Heathcliff's Garden,* Boston, MA   1986-88
Edited news stories, wrote headlines, assisted with layout of page. Occasionally solicited advertising and helped with distribution.

Other Experience
Writer, professional musician

Computer Skills
Operating Systems   DOS, Windows 2000, Macintosh
Writing/publishing   Word, WordPerfect, PageMaker
Business   Lotus 1-2-3

Military
Army Corporal (honorable discharge)

Education
Le Student Roma, Rome, Italy
Intensive study of Italian language and culture

University of Richmond, Richmond, VA
Bachelor of Arts in English

Because the dates are on the right and this person has stressed his/her experience, the gaps in employment history are no longer a stigma. You should, however, always have an answer ready to explain the gaps, no matter how deeply you buried them in your resume. The other factor working in this person's favor is that, despite the gaps, each position is one of more responsibility than the one before it. This shows the person moving in the right direction.

CHRIS SMITH
178 Green Street
Appleton, WI 54912
(414) 555-5555

Experience
UNITED STATES NAVY
Intelligence Specialist   1995-99
Served as intelligence analyst in photographic interpretation for FIRST at NAS Boston and Fleet
Intelligence Center Pacific. Participated in intelligence operations on month-long active duty assign-
ments. Edited and compiled contingency briefs for fleet surface ships at Commander Naval Surface
Force, Miami.

Intelligence Specialist   1991-95
Served as intelligence assistant at Commander Naval Surface Force, U.S. Pacific Fleet, Miami.
Edited and compiled point papers on foreign navies. Briefed shipboard intelligence officers on intel-
ligence collection effort.

Performed various other functions, including standing watch, serving as classified control custodian,
and clerical and editorial duties. Performed administrative duties in Special Security Office at Fleet
Intelligence Center Pacific, Los Angeles, CA.

Education
Marquette University, Milwaukee, WI   B.A. in Soviet Politics
Hamburg, St. Petersburg, Moscow, Paris   5-week study of Soviet languages

Military Training
National Imagery Interpretation Rating Scale School   Miami, FL
Shipboard Intelligence School   Miami, FL
Intelligence Specialists "A" School   Bangor, ME
Basic Training   Maui, HI

Languages
Fluent in German, French, Russian

Honors and Awards
Two Naval Certificates of Achievement

Clearance
Top Secret

The important thing to remember for people with a military background is
that you want to stress all relevant job information. In this case it's intelligence
gathering. For others it could be electronics, metal working, auto mechanic, leadership (officer), or many others.

CHRIS SMITH
178 Green Street
Johnson, VT 05656
(802) 555-5555

SUMMARY OF PROFESSIONAL EXPERIENCE
- Four years of substantial experience in positions as Sales Representative, Retail Sales Manager, and Warehouse Manager with retail and a major wholesale organization.
- Assumed responsibility for divisional sales from $1.4 million to $2.1 million within one year.
- Hands-on experience in sales, inventory control, and promotion of chemicals, furniture, clothing, and seasonal products.
- Skilled in developing special merchandising effects to increase product visibility and sales.

WORK HISTORY
Raintree, Inc.
Seasonal Specialty Stores, Raintree Industries, Johnson, VT

Retail Manager (part-time)   1997–present
- Hire, train, schedule, and supervise a highly productive staff of 11 selling and promoting a diverse product mix.
- Expand seasonal merchandise lines to develop year-round sales. Initiated use of in-store video and other image equipment to increase customer awareness of products.
- Select and purchase all billiard equipment and accessories.
- Create sales promotions (in-store and chain-wide) resulting in strong repeat business.
- Prepare inventory projections; maintain financial control of all debits/credits.

Wholesale Warehouse Manager, (part-time)   1996–1997
- Supervised a staff of six and controlled all aspects of shipping and receiving.
- Directed fleet scheduling maintenance as well as building maintenance control and security for this facility.

Sales Representative (part-time)   1995–1996
- Increased all aspects of wholesale pool and supply and accessory business.
- Supervised expanding sales and sales force.
- Established new sales and accounts within New England.

EDUCATION
Cornell University, Ithaca, NY
B.A. Business Administration

Part-time positions are often presented the same way you would full-time positions. Major accomplishments and skills are highlighted throughout the resume. One question does remain however: Why couldn't this person get a full-time job after graduating from college? If you're in this situation, you should *definitely* have answers ready for this question at the interview.

CHRIS SMITH
178 Green Street
Fairfax, VA 22030
(703) 555-5555

EXPERIENCE
Legal Assistant
Parnell & Swaggert
Fairfax, VA   1997-present
- Correspond via courier, telephone, letter, and facsimile with clients, attorneys, secretaries of state, U.S. Department of State, and foreign associates in matters of intellectual property law, primarily trademarks.
- Meet with clients regarding applications for and registration of trademarks.
- Duties also include compiling information from other Parnell & Swaggert branches, paying company's debit notes, and billing clients.

Legislative Intern
Office of Senator John Fisher
Washington, D.C.   Summer 1997
Handled legislative correspondence involving case work. Assisted Labor and Human Resources Committee, Judiciary Subcommittee, and Fund for a Democratic Majority. Projects included research, writing, and covering hearings.

Legislative Aide
Office of Senator Arthur Florio
Washington, D.C.   Summer 1996
Answered communications from constituents

COMPUTER SKILLS
Word, WordPerfect, Lotus 1-2-3

EDUCATION
George Mason University, Fairfax
BA, Law and Society

HONORS & AWARDS
- Oxford Honor Scholar
- Who's Who Among Students
- Student Government Award

Hey, a short employment history is a short employment history. This person has done a good job of filling out the resume with relevant computer skills, which are always a plus, and impressive honors and awards.

CHAPTER EIGHT

Writing Electronic Resumes

As time goes by, resumes are being read more by computers and less by people. So what does this mean for you, the first time resume writer? You may find yourself applying to an ad that tells you to send a scannable resume (a resume that can be read by a computer) or to send a resume via e-mail. Either way, you'll need to have a resume ready to go that can be read easily by a computer.

If you're still working out the resume basics from the preceding two chapters, then I wouldn't worry too much about electronic resumes just yet. I think it's a better idea to make sure you have a solid resume ready to go before you tackle this chapter. Also, you'll probably be applying for jobs that won't ask you to send an electronic resume. This chapter is just to give you the latest information on resumes. If you think you're ready to proceed, go for it!

Before you go ahead and throw out your old paper resume, be advised that not all companies stay up to speed on the latest technology. Many companies simply don't have the equipment to directly receive e-mailed resumes and search online databases for job candidates. Having a paper copy of your resume is still a necessity, especially since you'll need it to bring it with you to all those job interviews!

FORMAT

Keep your resume simple. The same elaborate formatting that makes your resume attractive to the human eye makes it impossible for a computer to understand. Your resume should be no longer than one page, except in unusual circumstances.

Abbreviations

Most resume scanning systems recognize a few common abbreviations, like BS, MBA, and state names, with or without periods. Widely used acronyms for industry jargon, like A/R and A/P on an accounting resume, are also generally accepted, although it's advisable to spell out most abbreviations on resumes. But if there's any question about whether an abbreviation is standard, play it safe and spell it out.

Paper

Don't bother with expensive paper. Use standard, twenty-pound, 8 1/2-by-11-inch paper. Because your resume needs to be as sharp and legible as possible, your best bet is to use black ink on white paper.

Typeface

Stick to the basics; this is no time to express your creativity. Choose a non-decorative font with clear, distinct characters, like Times or Helvetica. It's more difficult for a scanner to accurately pick up decorative fonts like script. Usually the results are unintelligible letters and words. A size of 12 points is ideal. Don't go below 10 points, as type that's too small may not scan well.

Style

Most scanners will accept boldface, but if a potential employer specifically tells you to avoid it, you can substitute all capital letters. Boldface and capitals are best used only for major section headings, like "Experience" and "Education." Avoid boldface for your name, address, and telephone number. It's also best to avoid italics or underlining, since this can make the words unintelligible.

Graphics, Lines, and Shading

Avoid the temptation to use lines and graphics to liven up what is an other-wise visually uninteresting resume. A resume scanner will try to "read" graphics, lines, and shading as text, resulting in computer chaos. Also avoid nontraditional layouts, like two-column formats.

White Space

Don't try to compress space between letters, words, or lines to fit everything on one page; this makes it more difficult for the computer to read. Leave plenty of space between sections.

Printing

Make sure the result is letter quality. The advice given for printing normal resumes still holds true. Avoid typewriters and dot matrix printers, since the quality of type they produce is inadequate for most scanners. Because your resume needs to be as sharp and legible as possible, always send an original, not a photocopy, and mail your resume rather than faxing it. For the same reason, in the unlikely event your resume is longer than one page, don't staple the pages together.

CONTENT

The information you include in your electronic resume doesn't really differ from a traditional resume; it's simply the manner in which you present it that changes. Traditionally, resumes include action verbs, like "managed," "coordinated," or "developed." Now, employers are more likely to do keyword searches filled with nouns, like degree held or software you're familiar with. Personal traits are rarely used in keyword searches by employers, but when they are, traits like team player, creative, and problem-solving are among the most common.

Keywords

Using the right keywords or key phrases in your resume is critical. Keyword searches tend to focus on nouns. Let's say an employer searches an employment database for a sales representative with the following keyword criteria: sales representative, BS/BA, exceeded quota, cold calls, high energy, willing to travel. Even if you have the right qualifications, if you don't use these keywords on your resume, the computer will pass over your application. To complicate matters further, different employers search for different keywords. These are usually buzzwords common to your field or industry that describe your experience, education, skills, and abilities.

Although there is no way to know for sure which keywords employers are most likely to search for, you can make educated guesses. Check help-wanted advertisements for job openings in your field. What terms do employers commonly use to describe their requirements? Job seekers in your field are another source, as are executive recruiters who specialize in your field. You'll want to use as many keywords in your resume as possible, but keep in mind that using the same keyword five times won't increase your chances of getting matched with an employer. Note, however, that if you're posting your resume to a job-hunting Web site, a small number of such sites rank resumes by the number of keywords and their frequency of occurrence. Your best bet is to find out ahead of time by reading the information on the site.

Name

Your name should appear at the top of the resume, with your address immediately underneath.

Keyword Summary

This is a compendium of your qualifications, usually written in a series of succinct keyword phrases that immediately follow your name and address. Place the most important words first on the list, since the computer may be limited in the number of words it will read.

Objective

As with traditional resumes, I don't recommend using a job objective. If you choose to use a job objective, try to keep it general, so as not to limit your opportunities. After all, while the computer does the initial screening, your resume will eventually be seen by a human hiring manager. Your objective should express a general interest in a particular field or industry ("an entry-level position in advertising") but should not designate a specific job title ("a position as a senior agency recruitment specialist"). Include a few keywords in the objective to increase your chances of getting matched ("a position as a financial analyst where I can utilize my on-the-job experience and MBA").

Experience and Achievements

Your professional experience should immediately follow the keyword summary, beginning with your most recent position. (If you're a recent college graduate, list your education before your experience.) Be sure your job title, employer, location, and dates of employment are all clearly displayed. Highlight your accomplishments and key responsibilities with dashes (in place of bullets on an electronic resume). Again, try to incorporate as many buzzwords as possible into these phrases.

Education

This section immediately follows the experience section. List your degrees, licenses, permits, certifications, relevant course work, and academic awards or honors. Be sure to clearly display the names of the schools, locations, and years of graduation. List any professional organizations or associations you're a member of; many recruiters will include such organizations when doing a keyword search.

References and Personal Data

Don't waste valuable space with statements like "References available upon request." Although this was standard fare for resumes of old, it won't win you any points on an electronic resume.

Don't include personal data, like your birthdate, marital status, or information regarding your hobbies and interests. Since it's unlikely these sections would include any keywords, they're only taking up space, and the computer will pass right over them.

POSTING YOUR RESUME VIA THE INTERNET

To remain truly competitive, your resume needs to be in a plain-text format you can send to employers and online databases electronically through cyberspace.

Converting Your Resume to a Plain-Text File

An electronic resume is sparsely formatted but is filled with keywords and important facts. If you've already prepared a resume that's computer-friendly, you don't have far to go to be able to post your resume on the Internet. A plain-text resume is the next step.

Instead of a Microsoft Word, WordPerfect, or other word processing document, save your resume as a plain-text, DOS, or ASCII file. These three terms are basically interchangeable; different software will use different terms. These words describe text at its most basic level, without formatting like boldface or italics. Furthermore, an ASCII document appears on the recipient's screen as left-aligned. If you have e-mail, your messages are written and received in this format. By converting your resume to a plain-text file, you can be assured it will be readable, regardless of where you send it.

Before you attempt to create your own plain-text resume, study the resumes on the online databases. This will give you a good idea of what a plain text resume looks like and will help you create your own.

Following are the basic steps for creating a plain-text resume. The particulars of the process will differ, depending on what type of computer system and software you're using:

1. Remove all formatting from your resume. This includes boldface, italics, underlining, bullets, different font sizes, lines, and any and all graphics. To highlight certain parts of your resume, like education or experience, you may use capital letters. You can also use hyphens (-) or asterisks (*) to emphasize certain accomplishments or experiences. Leave a blank line or two between sections.

2. Save your resume as a plain-text file. Most word processing programs, like Word and WordPerfect, have a "Save As" feature that allows you to save files in different formats. Some of your options in Word for Windows, for instance, are saving a document as a Word document, a text-only document, or a WordPerfect document. Many programs, like Word, don't specifically give you an "ASCII" option; in these programs, choose "Text Only" or "Plain Text." In Word, plain text files have the extension ".txt".

3. After saving your resume as a plain-text file, check the document with the text editor that most computers have. In Windows 3.1, use the Notepad from the Accessories group found in Program Manager. Open the file to be sure your margins look right and that you don't have extra spaces between lines or letters. If parts of the text are garbled with a group of strange characters, it is likely that you forgot to take out some formatting. A resume with a lot of formatting is likely to end up looking like hieroglyphs if it's read as a plain-text file. If this happens, go back to your original document and repeat the process.

4. Be sure all the lines contain sixty-five characters or fewer. This includes all spacing, letters, and punctuation. Often you will need to go through your entire resume line by line, counting each space, letter, punctuation, asterisk, and so forth. You may need to manually insert hard returns where the lines are longer than sixty-five characters. This may seem trivial, but it's actually extremely important. While some computers may recognize as many as seventy-five characters per line, the majority cannot recognize more than sixty-five characters.

5. Finally, e-mail your resume to yourself or a friend to test the file. Be sure it stays intact, that no extra spaces or returns are inserted during transmission, and that all text appears readable. If something doesn't look right, go back to your text editor, fix the problem, and test the resume again before e-mailing it to any companies or posting it to online databases.

E-mail

E-mailing your resume to potential employers is generally done in response to a help-wanted advertisement or simply as a method of direct contact. In fact, many companies now request that resumes be submitted through e-mail, rather than the U.S. mail or fax machine. Some job listings that you find on the Internet, particularly for technical positions, include only an e-mail address for contact information; no street address or telephone number is provided. With many companies, you can e-mail your resume directly into their in-house resume database. This eliminates the concern that it will be found unreadable by a computerized resume scanner. When e-mailing, paste your resume into the body of the message; many companies won't open an attachment because of the possibility that it may contain a computer virus.

After e-mailing your resume, wait a few days to be sure the recipient has read it. Call or e-mail the company to confirm that your resume was received intact. As with a paper resume, an e-mailed resume may do you little good unless you follow up to express your genuine interest. If you sent your resume to an individual, ask if he or she would like you to elaborate on any sections of your resume. If you sent it to a general e-mail address, call the human resources department to check the status of your application.

Online Resume Databases

Online resume databases are similar to electronic employment databases. These sites range from the general to the specific. Virtually all the major job-search sites on the Web, like CareerCity.com and Monster.com, offer resume databases. The Web contains dozens of sites for resume posting.

Most sites have instructions for entering a resume into their database. These instructions should tell you how long resumes remain in the database, how to update and remove your resume, who has access to the database, and the fee (if any). If a database doesn't have instructions, e-mail or call the site administrators for more information.

Some sites may require you to fill out personal information online, like your name, e-mail address, and resume title, but most allow you to attach your own resume or paste it in a specific area.

When e-mailing your resume to a database, don't overlook one important part of your e-mail: the subject line. This generally becomes your resume title, so it's important for it to give an indication of your field and job title. Many people mistakenly type "resume" or even their name on the subject line. The subject line is typically the first information seen by employers scanning the database and is often the only information a recruiter will look at. For this reason, it's important to be fairly specific on your subject line. Mention your profession, experience, and—since many resumes are seen by recruiters nationwide—your location. For instance, "Financial Analyst-3 yrs. exp.-CFA-IL." You could also mention if you're willing to relocate: "Financial Analyst-3 yrs. exp.-CFA-will relocate."

After e-mailing your resume to a database, try to download it. Once your resume is downloaded, make sure all the information is there and presented clearly. This serves a dual purpose. In addition to ensuring that your resume survived electronic transmission, conduct a keyword search to check that your resume turns up when appropriate. Be sure that downloading your resume is free before attempting this.

Major Resume Sites on the Web

Following are just some of the major job-search sites on the Web. These listings discuss only these sites' resume-posting capabilities, but many of these sites include a variety of other services that you may want to check out.

CareerCity
www.careercity.com

"The Web's Big Career Site" gives job hunters access to tens of thousands of jobs via three search engines: its own CareerCity jobs database; a newsgroup job-search engine covering hundreds of newsgroups; and addresses, phone numbers, descriptions, and hot links to 27,000 major U.S. employers. You'll find access to thousands of executive search firms and employment agencies, comprehensive salary surveys for all fields, and directories of associations and other industry resources. CareerCity's easy-to-use resume database gives job seekers the opportunity to market their qualifications free to employers subscribing to the database. The site is filled with hundreds of articles on getting started, changing careers, job interviews, resumes and cover letters, and more.

CareerMart
www.careermart.com

CareerMart's Resume Bank offers free resume postings to job seekers, and its E-mail Agent automatically notifies you when new positions crop up. Run by BSA Advertising, the site offers links to more than 400 major employers and some 700 colleges and universities. Resumes should be submitted as text files.

CareerMosaic
www.careermosaic.com

ResumeCM is CareerMosaic's database, which contains resumes from job seekers in all geographic areas and occupations. Besides the database on the Web, it also indexes the most popular Usenet newsgroups and automatically adds your resume to their databases. Unlike most databases, ResumeCM also allows employers to conduct a full-text search of your resume instead of searching only subject lines.

Career Shop
www.careershop.com

This site, produced by TenKey Interactive, enables you to post your resume and also e-mail it directly to employers free. Career Shop also offers a jobs database and allows employers who register with them to search the resume database free.

CareerSite
www.careersite.com

A free service of Virtual Resources Corporation, CareerSite's resume database allows you to submit your resume as a fully formatted document. You simply fill in some fields online to summarize your credentials. Information is presented to participating employers without your name and address, and your resume isn't released to a company without your consent—a great relief to job seekers concerned with confidentiality.

E-Span's JobOptions
www.joboptions.com/esp/plsql/espan_enter.espan_home
Available to employers nationwide, E-Span's JobOptions Resume Database allows you to enter your resume data into a section that formats the information for you, or you may paste in your resume as a plain text file.

JobBank USA
www.jobbankusa.com
Like E-Span, JobBank USA's resume database provides widespread exposure to employers nationwide and allows you to paste in your resume as a plain text file.

Monster.com
www.monster.com
Monster.com's Resume On-Line Database allows you to paste either plain text or HTML resumes. Monster.com protects applicants by keeping their personal information, including name and address, separated from the resume. Employers can access that information only after they've purchased the resume.

Commercial Online Services
In comparison to the Web, commercial online services, like America Online, CompuServe, Microsoft Network, and Prodigy, offer only limited resume posting services.

One exception is the Worldwide Resume/Talent Bank Service on America Online. This service is available through both America Online (keyword: Career Center) and the Internet, at the Internet Career Connection (www.icweb.com/resume). Besides full- or part-time help, many members have found consulting and volunteer work as well as positions on advisory boards. The service costs around $25 for a six-month subscription and accepts only plain-text resumes. To access the site through AOL, type in the keyword "Career Center," select the Gonyea Online Career Center, then select Resume Bank.

CHAPTER NINE

Creating an Effective Cover Letter

Your cover letter, like your resume, is a marketing tool. Too many cover letters are merely an additional piece of paper accompanying a resume, saying "Enclosed please find my resume." Like effective advertisements, effective cover letters attract an employer's attention by highlighting the most attractive features of the product. As with resumes, both the appearance, or format, of your cover letter and the content are important. These are discussed in separate sections below.

FORMAT

Before reading a word of your cover letter, a potential employer has already made an assessment of your organizational skills and attention to detail simply by observing its appearance. How your correspondence looks to a reader can mean the difference between serious consideration and dismissal. You can't afford to settle for a less than perfect presentation of your credentials. This chapter outlines the basic format you should follow when writing and shows you how to put the finishing touches on a top-notch product.

The Parts of a Letter

Your cover letter may be printed on the highest quality paper and typed on a state-of-the-art computer, but if it isn't arranged according to the proper format, you won't come across as a credible candidate. Certain guidelines apply when composing any letter.

Either of two styles may be used for cover letters: business style (sometimes called block style) or personal style. The only difference between them is that in business style, all the elements of the letter—the return address, salutation, body, and complimentary close—begin at the left margin. In personal style, the return address and complimentary close begin at the center line of the page, and paragraphs are indented.

Return Address

Your return address should appear at the top margin, without your name, either flush left or beginning at the center line, depending on whether you're using business style or personal style. As a rule, avoid abbreviations in the addresses of your cover letter, although abbreviating the state is acceptable. Include your phone number if you're not using a letterhead that contains it or it doesn't appear in it in the last paragraph of the letter. The idea is to make sure contact information is on both the letter and the resume.

Date

The date appears two lines below your return address, either flush left or centered, depending on which style you're using. Write out the date; don't abbreviate. Example: October 12, 2000.

Inside Address

Four lines beneath the date, give the addressee's full name. On subsequent lines, give the person's title, the company's name, and the company's address. Occasionally, the person's full title or the company's name and address will be very long and can appear awkward on the usual number of lines. In this case, you can use an extra line.

The body of the letter below the date should be centered approximately vertically on the page, so if your letter is short, you can begin the inside address six or even eight lines down. If the letter is long, two lines is acceptable.

Salutation

The salutation should be typed two lines beneath the company's address. It should begin "Dear Mr." or "Dear Ms.", followed by the individual's last name and a colon. Even if you've previously spoken with an addressee who has asked to be called by his or her first name, never use a first name in the salutation. In some cases, as when responding to "blind" advertisements, a general salutation may be necessary. In such circumstances, "Dear Sir or Madam" is appropriate, followed by a colon.

Complimentary Close

The complimentary close should be two lines beneath the body of the letter, aligned with your return address and the date. Keep it simple: "Sincerely," followed by a comma, suffices. Three lines under this, type your full name as it appears on your resume. Sign above your typed name in black ink.

Don't forget to sign the letter! As silly as it sounds, people often forget this seemingly obvious detail. An oversight like this suggests you don't take care with your work. To avoid this implication if you're faxing the letter and resume directly from your computer, you can type your name directly below the complimentary close, without any intervening space. Then follow up with a hard copy of the resume and the signed letter, with your name typed in the traditional place under the signature.

Enclosure

An enclosure line is used primarily in formal or official correspondence. It's not wrong to include it in a cover letter, but it's unnecessary.

Length

Three or four short paragraphs on one page is ideal. A longer letter may not be read.

Paper

Use standard 8 1/2-by-11-inch paper. A smaller size will appear more personal than professional and is easily lost in an employer's files; a larger size will look awkward and may be discarded for not fitting with other documents.

The same suggestions about paper for resumes also apply to cover letters. Remember to use matching paper for both your resume, cover letter, and envelope.

Typing and Printing

Your best bet is to use a word processing program on a computer with a letter-quality printer. Handwritten letters are not acceptable.

Don't try the cheap and easy ways, like photocopying the body of your letter and typing in the inside address and salutation. Such letters will not be taken seriously.

Envelope

Mail your cover letter and resume in a standard, business-sized envelope that matches your stationery. Unless your handwriting is extremely neat and easy to read, type your envelopes. Address your envelope, by full name and title, specifically to the contact person you identified in your cover letter.

CONTENT

Personalize Each Letter

If you are not responding to a job posting that specifies a contact name, try to determine the appropriate person to whom you should address your cover letter. (In general, the more influential the person, the better.) Try to contact the head of the department in which you're interested. This will be easiest in midsized and small companies, where the head of the department is likely to have an active role in the initial screening.

If you're applying to a larger corporation, your application will probably be screened by the human resources department. If you're instructed to direct your inquiry to this division, try to find out the name of the senior human resources manager. This may cut down on the number of hands through which your resume passes on its way to the final decision-maker. At any rate, be sure to include your contact's name and title on both your letter and the envelope. This way, even if a new person occupies the position, your letter should get through.

Mapping It Out

A cover letter need not be longer than three or four paragraphs. Two of them, the first and last, can be as short as one sentence. The idea of the cover letter is not to repeat what's in the resume. The idea is to give an overview of your capabilities and show why you're a good candidate for the job. The best way to distinguish yourself is to highlight one or two of your accomplishments or abilities. Stressing only one or two increases your chances of being remembered.

Be sure it's clear from your letter why you have an interest in the company; *many candidates apply for jobs with no apparent knowledge of what the company does!* This conveys the message that they just want any job. Indicating an interest doesn't mean telling every employer you have a burning desire to work at that company, because these statements are easy to make and invariably sound insincere. Indicating how your qualifications or experience meet their requirements may be sufficient to show why you're applying.

First paragraph

State the position for which you're applying. If you're responding to an ad or listing, mention the source.

Example:

> "I would like to apply for the position of research assistant advertised in the *Sunday Planet*" (or "listed on the Internet").

Second paragraph

Indicate what you could contribute to this company and show how your qualifications will benefit them. If you're responding to an ad or listing, discuss how your skills relate to the job's requirements. Don't talk about what you can't do. Remember, keep it brief!

Example:

> "In addition to my strong background in mathematics, I offer significant business experience, having worked in a data processing firm, a bookstore, and a restaurant."

Third paragraph

If possible, show how you not only meet but exceed their requirements—why you're not just an average candidate but a superior one. Mention any noteworthy accomplishments, high-profile projects, instances where you went above and beyond the call of duty, or awards you've received for your work. If you have testimonials, commendations, or evaluations that are particularly complimentary, you may want to quote a sentence from one or two of them.

Example:

> "In a letter to me, Dwayne Barry, president of NICAP Inc., said, 'Your ideas were instrumental to our success with this project.'"

Fourth paragraph

Close by saying you look forward to hearing from them. If you wish, you can also thank them for their consideration. Don't ask for an interview. If they're interested, they'll call. If not, asking won't help. Don't tell them you'll call them—many ads say "No phone calls." If you haven't heard anything in a couple of weeks, it probably means they're not interested, but a call is acceptable. (Expect to be politely brushed off.)

COVER LETTER BLUNDERS TO AVOID

The following list outlines some of the most common cover letter mistakes and ways to correct them. These examples have been adapted from real-life cover letters. Although some of these blunders may seem obvious, they occur far more often than one might think. Needless to say, none of the inquiries that included these mistakes met with positive results.

- *Listing unrelated career goals.* Don't say your ultimate goal is to be a professional guitar player if you're applying to be an accountant.
- *Using clichés and obvious comparisons* like "I am a people person," or "Teamwork is my middle name."
- *Using inappropriate stationery.* White and ivory are the only acceptable paper colors for a cover letter.
- *Sounding desperate.* "Please call today! I'll be waiting by the phone." "I really, really need this job to pay off medical bills." "I would sell my left kidney for an interview with your company!" "I AM VERY BADLY IN NEED OF MONEY!"
- *Confessing shortcomings* (one of the most common and damaging) "Although I have no related experience, I remain very interested in the management consultant position."
- *Forgetting to send the resume with the cover letter.*
- *Forgetting to sign the cover letter.*

Last, but not least, don't forget to proof your cover letter with care. Remember that the spell-checker on your computer won't notice mistakes like "too" when you mean "two." Have someone else read it too if you can.

RESPONSE TO A CLASSIFIED ADVERTISEMENT
(Administrative Assistant)

178 Green Street
Ecru, MS 38842
(601) 555-5555

November 1, 1999

Pat Cummings
Office Manager
Any Corporation
1140 Main Street
Chicago, IL 60605

Dear Mr. Cummings:

Your October 30 advertisement in the Jackson Review calls for an Assistant with a background rich in a variety of administrative skills, such as mine.

As an organized and detail-oriented individual with five years' experience in administration, I believe my qualifications match your requirements. My strengths also include independent work habits and superb computer skills.

As an Administrative Assistant at Lambert Hospital, I was in charge of all computer support, word processing and database, spreadsheet, and administrative functions. Duties included all purchasing, equipment maintenance, daily office operations, supervising of staff and volunteers, and coordinating various projects with staff and outside vendors.

I would appreciate the opportunity to discuss this position with you at your convenience, as it sounds like an exciting opportunity. If you have any questions, do not hesitate to contact me at the above-listed phone number or at (601) 444-4444.

Sincerely,

Chris Smith

Chris Smith

Enc. resume

RECENT GRADUATE (Legal Assistant)

178 Green Street
Aston, PA 19014
(215) 555-5555

April 4, 1999

Pat Cummings
Attorney-at-Law
Any Firm
1140 Main Street
Erie, PA 16563

Dear Mr. Cummings:

Justice Ellen Malone, of Allentown Courthouse, suggested that I contact you regarding an opening you may soon have for a Legal Assistant.

I will be graduating this May from Temple University with a Bachelor of Arts in African-American Studies. In addition to my core studies, I have studied in a variety of areas including business administration and computer applications. (In 1994, I was awarded the prestigious Lieberman Scholarship.) I also offer a strong background in law, having worked in a variety of legal settings throughout my college years. I was a volunteer for Temple's Student Legal Aid, helping students with a variety of legal problems. I worked part-time over the past three years as a Volunteer Probation Officer for the Allentown juvenile court. And in addition to being an Outside Media Contact for an Aston Outreach Unified Neighborhood Team, I spent one summer as a Research Assistant for the Chief County Clerk of Allentown.

All of these positions have given me a strong sense of the law and the American legal system. Moreover, this experience convinced me that I would like to pursue the law as a career. Justice Malone highly recommends your firm as one that might be a good match for my goals and qualifications.

I look forward to speaking with you, and thank you very much for your time.

Sincerely,

Chris Smith

Chris Smith

CHAPTER TEN

I Have an Interview, Now What?

Congratulations! Your terrific resume and cover letter have scored you an interview. Now what? Preparation is the key to successful interviewing. In a typical job search you will have very few interviews relative to the number of companies you contact. Interviews can be fun and exciting if you're fully prepared and have had a lot of practice.

COMPANY RESEARCH

Once you have an interview scheduled you must find out everything you possibly can about that company! Your efforts could make all the difference in distinguishing you from the competition. At the very least, determine the following about the firm at which you are interviewing:

> The principal products or services
> Their types of customers
> Their subsidiaries
> Their parent companies
> Their type of ownership
> Their approximate industry rank
> Their sales and profit trends
> Their announced future plans

To find this information, you will need to dig up every resource you can find. Remember in Chapter 3 when I discussed doing research on companies? You can use these same sources again to find out more detailed information. My favorite place is the World Wide Web. Company Web sites are great sources of information. For larger companies, you can call the investor relations department and request an annual report and search at the library for recent articles written about the company.

Your research may lead you to conclude that you don't want to work for the firm after all. If this happens, remember to *interview anyway.* You might come across something that changes your mind. You will definitely get more practice and improve your interview skills.

DRESSING FOR SUCCESS

How important is proper dress for a job interview? Well, the final selection of a job candidate will rarely be determined by dress. However, first-round candidates for an opening are often quickly eliminated by inappropriate dress. I am not suggesting that you rush out and buy a whole new wardrobe, but you should be able to put together an adequate interview outfit.

Top personal grooming is more important than finding the perfect outfit. Careful grooming indicates both thoroughness and self-confidence. Be sure that your clothes fit well and that they are immaculate, that your hair is neat and freshly washed, and that your shoes are clean and attractive. Women need to avoid excessive jewelry, makeup, or perfume. Men should be freshly shaven, even if the interview is late in the day.

ARRIVING ON TIME

As I noted earlier, people often arrive late for interviews. There are two major reasons for this: First, inexperienced candidates are likely to forget something or to take a little unplanned extra time to prepare. Second, they often underestimate how long it will take to get to the interview location.

Clearly, then, you must allow yourself plenty of time to get ready and travel to your job interview. You should not arrive at the interviewer's office more than ten minutes in advance. However, if you are driving across town, planning ten minutes of extra time is probably not enough. Plan to *get to the location at least thirty minutes early;* you can then spend twenty minutes in a nearby coffee shop or take a walk around the building. Interviews are important enough to build in a little extra time. Here's another tip: If you have never been to the interview location before, visit it the day before so you know exactly where you are going.

BEING POSITIVE

Many inexperienced job candidates kill their chances for a job by making negative comments during an interview. You should never make a negative statement about a former boss or teacher—even if it is completely true and fully justified.

You can greatly increase your chances of getting any job by projecting a positive, upbeat attitude during your job interview. This is one of the very best ways you can stand out from the competition. You can project this image by smiling from time to time during the interview; by responding to interview questions with enthusiasm; by demonstrating excitement about your past accomplishments; and by showing optimism about the prospect of starting your career.

HANDLING IMPOSSIBLE QUESTIONS

One of the biggest fears that job candidates harbor about job interviews is the unknown question for which they have no answer. To make matters worse, some recruiters may ask a question knowing full well that you can't possibly answer it!

Sometimes recruiters do ask seemingly impossible questions, just to see how you will respond. They usually don't ask such questions because they enjoy seeing you squirm in your seat; rather, they want to judge how you might respond to pressure or tension on the job. If you are asked a tough question that you simply can't answer, think about it for a few seconds. Then with a confident smile and without apology, simply say, "I don't know" or "I can't answer that question, but if I had to know it on the job, I would certainly find out."

Commonly Asked Interview Questions and Their Answers

The following responses to interview questions are listed as examples to show you how questions should be handled. They should not be used as the basis of "canned" or scripted answers. Adapt these responses for your own circumstances, but remember that, especially for college students or recent grads, how an answer is given can be more important than what is said. Be positive, project confidence, smile and make eye contact with the interviewer, listen carefully, and go with the flow!

Question: **Why didn't you get better grades in school?**
Answer: *I really enjoyed school and learning, but I tried to balance grades with activities and an active social calendar. Although grades were certainly important, I felt that at that time in my life, developing socially was just as important. Now of course, I'm more focused on my career.*

Question: **Where would you like to be in five years?**
Answer: *I plan to remain in the banking industry for the foreseeable future. I hope that within five years I will have developed a successful track record as a lending loan officer, first*

perhaps with consumer loans, but then switching to business loans. Ideally, I would hope that within five years I will also have advanced to servicing middle-market-size companies.

Question: **Did you enjoy your summer job as a dishwasher at Washington Street Grill?**

Answer: *I wouldn't want to do it for the rest of my life, but it was fine for a summer job. The work was more interesting than you might think, I enjoyed my co-workers, and I had a great rapport with my boss!*

Question: **Who was the toughest boss you ever had and why?**

Answer: *That would be Mr. Henson at Henson's Car Wash. He would push people to their limits when it got busy, and he was a stickler for detail. But he was always fair, and he went out of his way to be flexible with our work schedule and generous in advancing salaries when one of the kids was in a pinch. I would call him a tough boss, but a good boss.*

Question: **Tell me about a time when your employer was not happy with your job performance.**

Answer: *In the first week on the job there were two letters that had typos in them. Frankly, I had been a little sloppy with them. But that's all that comes to mind. Ms. Heilman did tell me on at least two occasions that she was very happy with my work.*

Question: **I see that while you returned to your hometown each summer you worked at a different company. Why didn't you work the same job two summers in a row?**

Answer: *My career goal is to get a job in business after graduation. Because I attend a liberal arts college, I can't take any courses in business. So, even though I was invited back to each summer job I held, I thought I could develop more experience by working in different positions. Although I didn't list high school jobs on my resume, I did work for almost three years at the same grocery store chain.*

Question: **Were you ever fired from a job?**

Answer: *Yes. I had a part-time courier job during my freshman year. I became violently ill with a stomach bug after lunch one day and had to call in sick thirty minutes before my shift began. I was immediately told that I was fired. I knew it was difficult for my boss to get a substitute courier on such short notice. But I was very dizzy and thought there would be too much risk of an accident if I reported to work.*

Question: **Have you thought about why you might prefer to work with our firm as opposed to one of the other firms to which you've applied?**

Answer: *Yes. I like your policy of promotion from within. I think the company's growth record is impressive, and I am sure it will continue. Your firm's reputation for superior marketing is particularly important to me because I want to pursue a career in marketing. Most important of all, it seems that your firm would offer me a lot of opportunities, not just for possible advancement but also to learn about many different product lines, all within one company.*

Question: **Tell me about yourself.**

Answer: *It takes me about thirty minutes in the morning to wake up but after that I'm all revved up and ready to go. I have a tremendous amount of energy, and love challenges at school, at work, and at home. This is true even when I'm performing mundane tasks, such as when I worked at the direct mail house last summer stuffing brochures into envelopes. I set up a challenge for myself to have the highest pace of anyone in the office, and I succeeded on every day but four during the entire summer. I also enjoy being around other people and working with them and doing anything I can to help the other people around me. For example, I really enjoyed tutoring freshmen in math. So while I push myself to high levels of performance and to achieve constantly more challenging goals, I try to remain sensitive to the concerns of people around me.*

AFTER THE INTERVIEW

Now that you've made it through the toughest part, what should you do? First, breathe a sigh of relief! Then, as soon as you've left the interview site, write down your thoughts about the interview while they're still fresh in your mind. Ask yourself key questions. What does the position entail? What do you like and dislike about the position and the company? Did you make any mistakes or have trouble answering any of the questions? Did you feel you were well prepared? If not, what could you do to improve your performance in the future? Carefully consider all of these questions; if you find that your performance was lacking, work to improve it.

Be sure to record the name and title of the person you interviewed with, as well as the names and titles of anyone else you may have met. Don't forget to write down what the next agreed-upon step would be. Will they contact you? How soon?

Writing Your Follow-Up Letter

Next, write a brief follow-up letter thanking the interviewer. You should do this immediately, within one or two days of the interview in order to make sure that you stay in the forefront of the recruiter's mind. The letter should be typewritten and no longer than one page. Express your appreciation for the opportunity to interview with the recruiter and your continued enthusiasm about the position and the company. Above all, make sure that the letter is personalized—don't send out a form letter! Remember to double check it for any typos! An example of a follow-up letter to send to an employer after a job interview follows.

When to Call

Allow the employer a week to ten days to contact you after receiving your letter. If you still haven't heard anything after this time, you should follow up with a phone call. Express your continued interest in the firm and in the position; inquire as to whether any decisions have been made or when you will be notified.

What's Next?

Don't be discouraged if you do not get an immediate response from an employer; most companies interview many applicants before making a final decision. The key is to remain fresh in the recruiter's mind. Beyond that, it's a waiting game.

But don't just sit by the phone! Take advantage of this time. Contact other firms and schedule more interviews so that if rejection does come, then you have other options open. This is a good idea even if you end up receiving a job offer, because you'll have a number of options to choose from and you'll be in a better position to make an informed decision. If you place too much importance on a single interview, you will not only waste time and energy, you will also increase the chances of a drop in your morale if the offer doesn't come through. So keep plugging!

Sample Follow-up Letter

460 Brook Road
Santa Fe, New Mexico 87541
505/555-5561

September 22, 1999

Joseph C. Barber
Director of Human Resources
Kendall Pharmaceuticals
11241 Sundown Drive
Albuquerque, New Mexico 87154

Dear Mr. Barber:

Thank you for the opportunity to discuss your opening for a statistician. I enjoyed meeting with you and Ms. Tate, Director, and learning more about Kendall Pharmaceuticals.

I believe that my experience at the Department of Labor and my educational background in statistics, economics, and business administration qualify me for the position. My extensive knowledge of computers and statistical software would also be especially valuable to me as a statistician with your firm.

I was particularly impressed with Kendall's strong commitment to innovation and growth, as well as its plans to expand into the overseas market. I feel that this type of environment would challenge me to do my best work.

I look forward to hearing from you within the next two weeks. In the meantime, please call me if I can provide more information or answer any questions to assist in your decision.

Sincerely,

Alison Ann Granville

Alison Ann Granville

Don't forget to sign your name!

THE JOB OFFER

Congratulations! You've gotten a job offer, or maybe even a few. What do you do now?

Let's start with some basic considerations. What is the minimum salary you can live on? What is the going rate in the current market for that particular position? Don't wait until you get to the offer stage to determine these figures, though; do it long before entering into negotiations with potential employers.

To consider the offer seriously, you should feel confident that this is a job you really want, that the field is one you'd like to pursue a career in, and that you are willing to live and work in the area in question. Ask yourself: is the lifestyle and work schedule associated with your potential new occupation one you would enjoy? Presumably you've had time to think about these issues and about whether this particular position satisfies your basic financial requirements.

Important Factors to Consider

Once you've received the offer, of course, you should have all the information about the position necessary for you in order to make a sound decision. This includes:

- start date
- job title and associated responsibilities
- potential for career progression
- salary, overtime, and compensation
- bonus structure
- tuition reimbursement or possible graduate studies
- vacation and parental leave policy
- life, medical, and dental insurance coverage
- pension plan
- job location
- travel

If you're unsure of any of this information, don't assume that it will be to your satisfaction. Contact the personnel representative or recruiting contact and confirm all important details.

Making Your Final Decision

Probably the most important thing to consider in evaluating an offer is whether you will be happy with the job and accomplish what is important to you. Don't accept a job because your friend works there or because a relative thinks it sounds great. Talk the offer over with other people, but trust your own reasoning ability. If you are confused, discuss your concerns with a career counselor and then make an informed decision based on what is right for you.

INDEX